To order additional copies of
Brushed Back,
by Ethan and Mardene Fowler, call **1–800–765–6955**.

Visit us at
www.reviewandherald.com
for information on other Review and Herald® products.

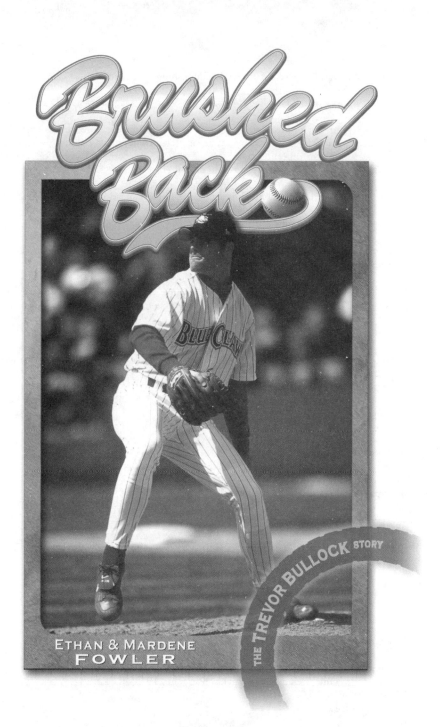

Brushed Back

ETHAN & MARDENE
FOWLER

THE TREVOR BULLOCK STORY

REVIEW AND HERALD® PUBLISHING ASSOCIATION
Since 1861 | www.reviewandherald.com

Published by Review and Herald® Publishing Association, Hagerstown, MD 21741-1119

Review and Herald® titles may be purchased in bulk for educational, business, fund-raising, or sales promotional use. For information, e-mail SpecialMarkets@reviewandherald.com

The Review and Herald® Publishing Association publishes biblically based materials for spiritual, physical, and mental growth and Christian discipleship.

The author assumes full responsibility for the accuracy of all facts and quotations as cited in this book. To protect privacy, some names have been changed and some conversations and/or situations have been enhanced or created.

Unless otherwise noted, Bible texts are from the *Holy Bible, New International Version*. Copyright © 1973, 1978, 1984, International Bible Society. Used by permission of Zondervan Bible Publishers.

Scripture quotations marked NLT are taken from the *Holy Bible*, New Living Translation, copyright © 1996. Used by permission of Tyndale House Publishers, Inc., Wheaton, Illinois 60189. All ights reserved.

This book was
Edited by Jeannette R. Johnson
Designed by Ron J. Pride
Cover photography/David M. Schofield
Interior designed by Heather Rogers
Typeset: Bembo 11.5/14

PRINTED IN U.S.A.

13 12 11 10 09   5 4 3 2 1

Library of Congress Cataloging-in-Publication Data
Fowler, Ethan, 1971-
  Brushed back : the story of Trevor Bullock / Ethan and Mardene Fowler.
    p. cm.
1. Bullock, Trevor—Juvenile literature. 2. Seventh-Day Adventists—United States—Biography—Juvenile literature. I. Fowler, Mardene, 1973- II. Title.
  BX6193.B85F69 2009
  286.7092—dc22
  [B]
                                              2008052465

ISBN 978-0-8280-2420-4

ACKNOWLEDGMENTS

The path to completing a book such as this is long. First, the story has to actually happen and be shared. Then it gets filtered through the thinking and experiences of the writers. Then when story meets author and the book meets publisher, there are a multitude of people who deserve to be thanked.

We are deeply grateful to Trevor and Carissa Bullock for their time and patience during long phone interviews. Their honesty and vulnerability made this book a reality.

We appreciate the friends, family, and coaches who gave of their time: Duaine and Ardyce Bullock, Aaron Madsen, Nate Lueders, Rob Childress, Guy Murray, Bob Steinkamp, Chad Sadowski, Rob Avila, Kelly Krueger, and Richard Spaulding.

Key information was obtained through the efforts of Peter Yazvac (University of Nebraska-Kearney) and Shamus McKnight (University of Nebraska-Lincoln) of the Sports Information Departments; and Brendan Burke, Lakewood BlueClaws media and public relations manager.

Guide magazine editor, Randy Fishell, exhibited incredible patience in dealing with a couple novice writers. We can't thank him enough for his continued encouragement and long-suffering attitude.

Friends Mike Jones, David Wilkening, and Mandy Flynn (all accomplished writers) saw an embarrassingly early draft. Mike covers the Washington Wizards for the Washington *Times*; David is an adjunct English and journalism professor and freelance travel story writer from Orlando, Florida; and Mandy is a columnist and former features editor from Albany, Georgia. They were generous with their time and constructive in their critique.

Throughout our lives there have been people who believed in our ability to write: Ethan's former teachers, Tim Curtis and Randolph "Ran" Hennes, and the staff in the writing help center at the University of Washington's Education Opportunities Program;

and Mardene's former teachers, Carolyn Howson, Pam Tait, and Ila Zabaraschuk. Often they've been passionate and pointed in their assessment. (Without them we probably couldn't have even formed a complete sentence.)

Ethan's journalistic endeavors took root in the Fowler home. His father, Emery; mother, Elaine; and siblings, Emery, Jr., Elisa, Eliot, Evans, Egan, and Everett were supporters and observers along the way. Elaine helped edit stories and enjoyed coming up with headline ideas during Ethan's early years as a writer.

Walla Walla University professors Alden Thompson and Dan Lamberton truly deserve a medal for their efforts with Mardene. They taught Research Writing in Religion, a class intended to prepare a student for writing books for religious publishers, such as those published by the Review and Herald Publishing Association. Mardene never intended to write for such a publisher and spent most of the class in a foul mood. She now wishes to apologize.

Ethan's writing has been significantly enhanced by the unwavering diligence of his editors and fellow writers: Jay Maebori of the University of Washington's *The Daily*; Mark Briggs of the *Northshore Citizen*; Greg Johns, Dan Ivanis, Tom Moore, and Mike Moore of the *Journal American/Eastside Journal*; Steve Kelley of the Seattle *Times;* Jane Meyer of the *Mercer Island Reporter*; Lou Emerson of the Fauquier *Citizen*; and Dee Maret, Jim Hendricks, and Danny Carter of the Albany *Herald*.

In the fall of 2002 Ethan made the difficult decision to join the Seventh-day Adventist Church. It meant giving up his sports writing career. In the midst of our uncertainty about what the future held for us, Mardene's mother sent us a copy of Amanda Sauder's story about Trevor Bullock from the September 19, 2002, issue of *Adventist Review*. Because Trevor's story had many parallels to our life at the time, we felt a certain connection to him, and saved Amanda's article. Little did we know that several years later God would open to us this opportunity. Thank you, Amanda, for introducing us to Trevor Bullock!

In the months and years that have followed Ethan's decision to join the Adventist Church, we've been greatly blessed with wonderful friends. These friends have prayed for us, listened to us, studied the Bible with us, and stood by us when there were far more questions than answers: Jeff and Wendi Rogers, Hans and Julie Fairbank, Garth and Lani Woodruff, Bruce Cameron, Kellie Rodman, Pastor Joey Pollom, Matt and Christa Demaree, and Pastor Steve Rose.

We each were brought to Christ when we were children. As we grew up there were people who touched our lives with their love and encouraged us to continue in our walk of faith. These people are particularly special to us and have made a memorable contribution to our spiritual thoughts and growth:

- Mardene's devoted parents, Dale and Louise Bartholomew.
- Mardene's brother, Cameron Bartholomew.
- Ethan's youth teacher, Dan Powell, at Queensgate Baptist Church.
- Ethan's friend, Tony Cothrum, and the staff of the Baptist Student Union at the University of Washington.
- Pastors Jess and Ginny Nephew at Sunset Lake Camp, Maylan Schurch at the Bellevue Seventh-day Adventist Church, and the Reverend Caroline Smith-Parkinson at Grace Episcopal Church.
- Mardene's friends: Sherilyn (Harms) Carlton, Becky (Guth) Colvin, Ruth Christensen, Aletha (Sharer) Natiuk, Alvin Wolcott, Bob Thayne, James Ash, Dawn Lloyd, Shem Bingman, Julie Carlson, and Melody Blufton.
- Mardene's teachers, John and Dorothy Zollbrecht, Gloria Henry, Althea (Hamilton) Wright, Diane Brateng, Rob and Carolyn Howson, Doug White, Pam Tait, Orlin McLean, Tom Allen, Carolyn Withrow, Brandon and KarrLayn Beck, Loren Dickinson, Bruce Johanson, Alden Thompson, Ernie Bursey, Larry Veverka, Pedrito Maynard-Reid, Glen Greenwalt, Doug Clark, and Ron Jolliffe.
- Church members Harley Wellman, Marion Burtt, Elaine Lester, Duane and Emily Childs, Jim and Sheryl Learned, George and Nona Nordby, Mike and Carol Wade, Bob and

Colette Sharer, Jeanette Salsman, Molly Morin and her parents, James and Lisa Morin, Bobby and Melanie Jackson, Mary Lavoie, and Betty Ramsey.

- Additionally, we wish to thank the Reverend Rollin Stierwalt for officiating at our wedding and bestowing on us God's blessing, even though we were relative strangers. Pastor Stierwalt truly made our life together—and ultimately the writing of this book—possible.

-Finally, we thank God for choosing us to do this work. He has blessed us with a colorful and often humbling life. We thank Him for persistently calling us to walk with Him. The blessing has been all ours as we've witnessed the redeeming work of God in Trevor Bullock's life.

INTRODUCTION

Duaine Bullock was an athlete. It all came pretty easy for him. He played basketball and baseball. He did track and field. And he was an all-state football player at Dorchester High. He went to Kearney State College in Kearney, Nebraska, but school wasn't his thing. So he dropped out and joined the Marine Corps. Eventually he served his country in Vietnam.

While home on leave he met Ardyce Bechthold, who was dating one of his friends. She was a bright and friendly girl, a little strict about her religion perhaps, but he liked her. Ardyce, a fifth-generation Seventh-day Adventist, had attended Union College in Lincoln, Nebraska, and held a degree in social welfare.

The two hit it off. He was a handsome one. (She thought his dark hair was alluring.) He liked her outgoing spirit, and she liked his quiet, steady, no-nonsense demeanor. He was very kind—but you didn't always know it.

They were married in May 1971. They didn't plan on having children; nevertheless, Trevor Duaine Bullock made his entrance into the world nearly six years later.

Trevor was a "marvelous oops," Ardyce said, a boy filled with marvelous talent and drive. And he was a boy who fell into one "oops" after another as he learned the lessons of life the hard way.

What follows is his story.

Chapter 1

Three hours before game time Trevor strode into the white-washed training room. He strutted on the balls of his feet, just like his father, Duaine, used to walk. His perfectly cropped brown hair, meticulously trimmed sideburns, and hint of a goatee exuded an aura of a cocky jerk. He was handsome, and he knew it.

As he rounded the corner he heard Gene Kurtz talking smack about Anna Boutwell. "Yeah, right!" he muttered under his breath. Anna was beautiful, and most of the guys *wanted* the chance to be in the same room with her, but Trevor was one of the only ones who actually had the confidence to speak to her. Trevor had never seen Gene anywhere near Anna.

"I'm tellin' ya, Anna wants me," boasted the sandy-haired center fielder. "I can totally see it in the way she looks at me, especially the way she's always touching her hair around me. That's a total giveaway! She digs me," he said, nodding his head confidently.

Gene had recently moved to the area from Minnesota. One couldn't blame him for trying to seem cool to all his new teammates, but the pretty girls were Trevor's turf, and he wasn't about to concede even one flutter of an eyelash to some other hopeful male.

"So you think Anna wants you?" Trevor scoffed, perching on the edge of a table. "Who are you kidding? Anna doesn't like you! She's probably scratching her head, trying to figure out how to get away from you." Looking bored, Trevor gave his head the slightest questioning shake. "Do you hear yourself, Gene? Anna thinks you're an idiot! She's told me so tons of times. She told me so *today* at lunch."

Gene launched himself from the bench and thundered, "Bullock, you need to shut your piehole before I shut it for you!"

Trevor looked up. "Are you trying to scare me, Gene?" he said indifferently. "Because you don't." He looked through Gene as though he wasn't even there.

It was infuriating. "You arrogant piece of trash!" Gene screamed. Raising his fist, he sent it crashing into Trevor's mouth, knocking him off the table.

The mineral taste of blood immediately flowed over Trevor's tongue, and he could feel one of his teeth protruding through his lower lip. A moment of stunned silence filled the locker room.

At the sight of blood Gene's face switched from rage to panic as he realized that he had just sucker punched the team's stud pitcher. "Oh, man! Oh, *man!* Trevor, are you OK? I'm sorry, dude. I didn't mean to—"

"Oh, shut up already, Gene!" Trevor spat a mouthful of the thickening blood into a towel.

"Dude, I'm taking you to the hospital!" Gene blurted. Because of his unchecked fist he knew he might lose his starting center field position, maybe get kicked off the team.

"Well, if you're thinking of taking me to the hospital you might want to do it now!" Trevor seethed.

Gene reached out his hand to help him up and offered to steady him with his shoulder, but Trevor pushed him aside. "It's my lip you broke, you idiot, not my legs. I can walk to my car. It's a good thing you did this while Coach McLaughlin wasn't around; otherwise, you might not be walking yourself!"

As the two approached Trevor's Chevy Z24 Cavalier coupe, Trevor tossed the keys underhand to Gene and continued to rant. "As you know all too well, I *am* this team. Without me this team would be *nothing*. Our best chance of getting anywhere this postseason is with my left arm—and you staying out of my way."

This wasn't actually true. Trevor's best friend, Aaron Madsen, was also an impressive lefty pitcher. Many people thought Aaron was even better than Trevor. But what use was the truth when Trevor was mad?

Gene leaned across the front seat and pushed open the passenger door. Trevor slumped into the seat, his frustration nearly spent. "By the way, did I tell you you're an idiot?"

Gene didn't respond. He was already threading the car out of the parking lot and into traffic.

At the emergency room entrance a technician met them and gave Trevor a perfunctory once-over. "Hey," she said, "I think I know you . . ." She grinned. "You're always in the paper—aren't you one of Southeast's awesome lefty pitchers? You always look like you're about to stuff the baseball down the batter's throat or something."

"Well, it's nice to know somebody still reads the Lincoln *Journal Star*," Trevor said dryly. He was not in the mood for this. "Seems like I sure have to answer a lot of stupid questions from all those flabby, soft, wannabe sportswriters. So, hey, it's nice to finally meet someone who actually follows high school baseball."

"I only follow Lincoln Southeast. My little sister goes there. And I graduated from there five years ago," the technician stated matter-of-factly. She motioned Trevor into an examining room and added, "You're in luck! We're not that busy, so we'll get you patched up before any of your girlfriends miss you!" she teased. Then she took Gene by the arm and led him to the waiting area. Leaning toward Gene, she advised, "You might want to call your coach."

"I might not," Gene muttered under his breath as he flopped into a chair. He could hear Trevor in the examining room, shouting to no one in particular, "Hey, I'm the starting pitcher for Southeast. We play against Northeast High at Sherman Field in less than an hour. C'mon, folks, let's get moving! It's the first round of playoffs!" Sliding deeper into the chair, Gene began to hope the doctor would stitch Trevor's punky lips all the way shut.

Fifteen minutes and six stitches later, Trevor and Gene sped back to Sherman Field.

"We've got to hurry up!" Trevor yelled. "Pretty soon my mom is going to freak out, and my dad will send the whole Lincoln police force out looking for me."

They shot into a parking space, and Trevor sprinted to the locker room to grab his mitt. Gene lagged behind. He was in no hurry to face Coach McLaughlin. The rest of the team was already on the field warming up, and he could see that Steve Rivera was in center field. He'd be watching his team today. He found a seat in the dugout and rested his chin in his hands.

Trevor saw Aaron warming up on the mound. With their matching build and dark hair, people often commented that the two bore a striking resemblance to each other. Aaron might be the better pitcher, but seeing him on the field made Trevor unhappy. He really wanted to pitch this game. "Hey, Coach! There's nothing to worry about!" he insisted. "The doctor stitched me up, and I'm good to go! This is my start."

"OK, Trevor," McLaughlin conceded, "but I'm not going to let this game get away from you."

From her seat near the dugout Trevor's mom heard her son confront the coach. She stepped closer and held him in a worried, penetrating stare. "Stitched you up? What happened?" she demanded.

"You mean nobody told you?" Trevor was surprised and, frankly, a little hurt. Nobody was talking about what happened? The team's best pitcher gets his lip busted and nobody is even talking about it? He shook his head in frustration. "Listen, Mom, don't worry about it. I've got to go warm up now. I'm fine, and I'm going to send Northeast home in a hurry," he called over his shoulder as he headed to the mound.

Ardyce went back to the bleachers. She had come straight to the game from her job at College View Seventh-day Adventist Church. So no, she hadn't heard any talk of Trevor's afternoon. His lip looked awful, and she was going to worry whether he liked it or not.

As he ran onto the field Trevor hoped his dad wouldn't blow a gasket over the whole thing. It wasn't always all that great having a cop for a dad, sort of an enforcer in the middle of his life trying to solve all his problems.

But none of that mattered now. He wanted to focus. Turning to the catcher, he threw the ball. *Hard.* "Hey!" Nate yelled. Nate Leuders had played catcher with Trevor since they'd been small. Stocky, and with a penchant for smart-aleck commentary, he was also Trevor's cousin.

"So the two ladies' men were fighting over a girl," Nate cracked. "No surprise there!" He stroked the small accumulation of fuzz on his chin. "It was Huggy Bear trying to fend off David Hasselhoff. I hope neither one messed up his hair."

Trevor ignored him and continued loosening up his arm.

Coach McLaughlin jogged out to the mound to check on Trevor. "I'm not happy about what happened," he boomed. "And I want you to know that Gene's on the bench. As far as I'm concerned he can stay there until the bench rots." McLaughlin kicked some dirt to make his point. "What a fool! Anyway, Steve's playing center now." He thumped Trevor's shoulder a couple times, then trotted back to the dugout.

Trevor surveyed the scene from the mound. It was a warm Nebraska spring day, and the crowd was dressed in the lightweight clothing of summer. He noticed a couple girls from Northeast High. No matter where he was, he sure could spot the hot babes. Catching himself, Trevor turned back toward the black-and-gold colors of the Lincoln Southeast stands and found his girlfriend, Sam. She really was beautiful! And she drove a cute little two-seater BMW. (Her dad owned the dealership.)

"OK, man, you can take these guys!" Nate had arrived on the mound for a last-minute pregame chat. "A lot of these guys were behind your pitches the last time we played. And now your changeup and curve-ball are coming around. You can get them with your fastball, too. This is going to be another great performance for you. . . . Maybe you'll have a chance to get the digits for that blond over there in the pink halter top." Nate gestured toward the Northeast stands. "I saw you checkin' her out. If you want her kisses, you've gotta focus on my mitt." Nate gave Trevor a silly grin. "My mitt, her number. It's that easy."

"OK, I gotcha." Trevor gave him a shove back toward the plate. "Trust me, I'm focused. Get your fat behind back to the plate, and let's get this thing going!" The afternoon had been long enough; he was done listening to Nate's wisecracks.

Trevor stepped onto the mound. He put on his game face—like an angry pit bull. Nate flashed the signal for a fastball up and in, and Trevor nodded. Northeast's leadoff hitter was Joey Raines, a left-handed batter who struck a wiggly pose, bat and hips shifting side to side. Trevor's fastball sailed right by him for a strike.

Raines scowled. He hated Trevor's windup. He hated the way Trevor turned his back on the batter before uncorking the ball. Pulling his batting helmet down a little farther, he fixed Trevor with an icy stare. Trevor looked in for the sign. An outside curveball. Raines's bat sliced the air violently as Trevor's pitch landed in Nate's glove with a hearty *thwop!* Strike two.

Frustrated, Raines stepped out of the batter's box and glared at Trevor before turning to the third-base coach for a sign. The coach signaled for a bunt. Raines didn't want to bunt. He wanted to rip Trevor's pitch to outer space. He shook his head and looked back at the coach. Still a bunt.

Raines stepped back into the box. He turned and squared for the bunt—and nearly fell on his face as he reached for Trevor's pitch, low and outside.

"*Steeee-RIKE!*" the umpire bellowed, sending Raines back to the dugout.

Trevor was on fire. He retired 18 of the next 20 batters, and walked two. He had 10 strikeouts heading into the last out of the game. Southeast carried a slim 2-0 lead, and Trevor's blood was pumping in anticipation of his first high school no-hitter.

He stepped off the mound and looked around. He wasn't going to rush himself with this final hitter. As he looked toward the first baseline, he saw his dad occupying his usual space. Duaine Bullock was an intimidating force. A dominating, no-nonsense kind of man, he'd been on the Lincoln police force for more than 30 years, the past 10 as captain of the narcotics division. He'd been a high school pitcher himself, and he sensed Trevor's nervousness. He whistled and raised his chin in a sign for Trevor to focus and take care of business.

Trevor caught his cue. Well, all right. He'd have to try to keep his cool. Stepping back on the mound, he cocked his head and shook out his shoulders. Judging by the ever-rising chatter of cheers and clapping, he knew he had the crowd's attention.

Eddie Larkin had smacked eight home runs so far this season. He'd flown out deep to center and left field on his two prior at bats. Trevor *was* nervous about Larkin, and Nate sensed it. He called a timeout and ran out to the mound. He didn't want some wiry punk with fantastic bat speed to get into his cousin's head. It was obvious that Trevor was feeling the pressure of being one out away from a no-hitter. And the buzz of anticipation coming from the crowd wasn't helping.

"Hey, forget about the no-hitter," Nate told him. "It's not worth worrying all this much for. Remember, wins mean more than no-hitters. Just take care of business, and we'll talk history later."

"Look, I know what's on the line. I also know what a good story my no-hitter would make for the Lincoln media types," Trevor retorted. "Just get back behind the plate, and let's get this over with."

Larkin kicked at the dirt in the batter's box. He bent his knees and sneered at Trevor. "C'mon, pretty boy, give me your fastball!" he begged under his breath.

Trevor pretended not to notice Larkin's antics. He sent him an outside curveball. Larkin ripped it foul along the third baseline for a strike. Undaunted, Larkin glowered at Trevor and stayed in the batter's box.

Nate signaled an inside changeup, and Trevor delivered. Larkin swung well ahead of the pitch. Strike two. The Lincoln Southeast fans roared with glee and stood up in unison to support Trevor in his no-hitter bid. They began stomping their feet on the metal stands, chanting "Bull-*ock!* Bull-*ock!* Bull-*ock!*"

Northeast coach Don Stancy had seen enough. Motioning to the umpire for a timeout, he called Larkin back toward the dugout. "Now, you know what he likes to pitch in this situation!" Stancy barked. "His strikeout pitch is the down-and-away fastball. You practiced hitting that pitch yesterday. You can do this—he's hittable, so just relax and nail him!"

Larkin walked back to home plate.

Trevor looked in for Nate's sign: a circle changeup. Trevor was tempted to shake him off. He'd just thrown a changeup. Was it really such a good idea to send one in again? He wasn't sure. But Nate had been calling this no-hitter so far, and Trevor decided to go with him. The ball came in smooth and slow. Larkin swung with all his strength and spun all the way around before Trevor's pitch even made it to Nate's glove.

A no-hitter! Turning toward first base, Trevor pumped his fist toward his dad.

"Oh, you got the ladies tonight, don't you, big boy!" Nate teased as he ran out to bump chests with Trevor. Then they were engulfed in a celebrating flood of Southeast players and coaches.

"I should punch him in the lip before every game," Gene muttered as he stalked back to the locker room.

Chapter 2

Trevor may have finished off his senior year at Lincoln Southeast High with a dramatic no-hitter in baseball, but things had been shaping up much differently that summer before his senior year. Then, everybody thought he'd be Southeast's starting quarterback. He had the charisma and arm to lead the Knights into the playoffs. . . .

"Boy, it must be nice to be the big man on campus," Trevor's dad said, giving him a punch in the chest. They were watching an afternoon preseason football game between the Kansas City Chiefs and Washington Redskins. "I mean, you can have any girl you want, right?"

"You got that right," Trevor agreed with a wide grin. "The chicks dig me. I'm *the* starting quarterback. And they like me for my body."

"Oh, for cryin' out loud!" Duaine snorted, rolling his eyes. "Listen, to be truly ready for this coming year you've gotta get your head in gear. You've gotta lead your team and make plays as the quarterback. This isn't about how many passes you can make with the ladies. You got it?"

"Chill out, Dad," Trevor sulked. "I've got everything under control. There's nothing to worry about—I've been training for this for a long time." He'd always liked football and was looking forward to the coming season. "I'll make you and Mom proud. Just wait and see."

"Well, you better," Duaine grumbled. "The guys down at the station think you're going to fall flat on your face leading the Knights this season. Spriger said your line is so weak you'll probably get sacked too often to show off your arm." Duaine drew in his breath for what Trevor could only guess would be a solemn concluding note. "I just don't want you to hurt that pitching arm. It's your only hope of getting out of here."

Hoping to calm his father's worries, Trevor said, "Look, Dad, don't sweat it. I'll be fine." Then, switching gears, he asked, "You wanna play some catch? Let me go get the football."

As they stepped out into the late-afternoon sun, Trevor felt just a little more free. This was his space, his neighborhood. He'd grown up in this small brick house on the cul-de-sac. The front yard was their place, just his dad and him. He hoped a little diversion would take the preaching tone out of his dad's voice. It got so old having his parents worry about him all the time.

They had tossed the ball around for about 20 minutes when Trevor's mom came to the door, the cordless phone in her hand. "Trevor, Seth's on the phone!" she called.

"Hey, Dad, can we pick this up later, maybe after I get off the phone?" Trevor asked.

"Sure. Yeah, that's fine," Duaine replied. He wiped a trickle of sweat off his forehead. "When you get done you can find me in the basement watching the Chiefs whip the Redskins."

Trevor took the phone from his mom and waved her back into the house. He wanted to take this call alone on the porch. "Hey, what's up? I know you wouldn't call me unless you have something going on."

"Well, some of the guys are going over to James's house," Seth reported. Seth was the starting center for the Knights football team and was usually in the know about any good gatherings. "His parents are out of town, and we wanted to chill out. You in?"

"Yeah, I'm in," Trevor said. "See you in about five minutes."

He breezed into the house. "Dad!" he yelled. "I'm going to hang out with Seth. We'll be at James's house. The plan is to go over some plays and then go out for pizza later."

"How much later?" Duaine shouted back from the basement. "I don't want you out too long, you know. I still expect you to keep your grades up."

"I'll be home by 8:30. We can watch a little of the Sunday night football game on ESPN before I wrap up my homework and hit the sack. See ya, Mom," Trevor called to Ardyce in the general direction of the kitchen.

He headed to his bedroom to collect his keys and wallet before dashing out the front door to his car. As he drove the few blocks to James's house, Trevor smiled smugly at himself in the rearview mirror. It was so easy to feed his parents some line and get out of the house. For being the narcotics captain, his dad sure was trusting.

"Do you know this Seth very well?" Ardyce asked Duaine. She had her back to him, intentionally trying to look relaxed as she leaned against the back of the couch. If the truth were known, she was afraid to look at him, afraid that if she saw anxiety in his face it would make her feel worse. "It's just that he's been going out a lot with people I've never met before, people he says he plays sports with." Finally turning toward Duaine she sighed wearily. "I don't like how he seems to know just what to say to get out of the house."

Without taking his eyes off the TV, Duaine forced a little bravado into his voice. "Don't worry; our son's a good kid. Sure, he has some wild and rough friends—what popular kid doesn't? But Trevor has a good head on his shoulders." He flashed her a grin. "Besides, he's going to James's house. We've known James since he was a kid. It'll be fine."

Ardyce nodded and trudged up the stairs. He was probably right. Even so, she wished Trevor was going to Aaron's house. Aaron really did seem like a nice kid. James was a different story . . .

As if reading her thoughts, Duaine called after her, "But just to be sure, I'll have one of my division's unmarked cars swing by there in an hour."

Any comfort he thought to give her evaporated. Maybe there really was something to be worried about. Trevor may have been her "marvelous oops," but right now there didn't seem to be much that felt marvelous about parenting him.

Trevor pulled into the driveway of a two-story Tudor, surrounded by a meticulously manicured lawn. In stark contrast to the order of the lawn, James and Seth came staggering out of the house. Clearly James's parents had better control over their yard than they had over their son.

"Guys!" Trevor chided. "Did you have to go dipping into the fun before I even got here?"

The pair guffawed raucously. Their pupils were already weirdly dilated. Behind them a cheerleader named Sara appeared at the door.

"Now, wait just a minute!" Trevor's voice took on an edge of irritation. "You had Sara over here and didn't invite me until *now?*"

"Dude, we wanted some time with the girls by ourselves," Seth retorted. Then looking perplexed, he turned to James and tilted his head sideways. "I did get to have some fun with the girls, didn't I?" he asked in a dazed tone.

Trevor rolled his eyes. It was obvious that both guys were totally wasted. He put his arm around Sara and walked into the house. Rachael, a tall, athletic blond from the volleyball team, was sprawled across the couch. She had already lost her shirt somewhere, and wore only a black bra and Calvin Klein jeans. A joint dangled from her fingers. "H-i-i-i, Trevor!" she cooed.

Jennifer, sitting beside her, licked on a big spiral lollipop. Other teenagers lay around the room in various stages of intoxication.

Trevor scooted up to Rachael. "Are there any other football players here? I came to talk about some plays," he said.

Rachael giggled. "I knew it wouldn't take long for you to be beggin' for some plays. Here; have some of my weed, and then you and I can make some plays of our own," she breathed into his ear, holding her joint up so he could take a draw.

Trevor shoved her back down onto the couch. "Oh, c'mon, Rach. I didn't come here to make out. Not tonight. And not with you. You're James's girl—in case you forgot." He took her joint and drew in one slow, sweet breath of pleasure before handing it back. It felt good to relax. And there didn't appear to be any other football players around to talk with anyway.

After a few hours Trevor headed home. As he pulled into the driveway, he glanced at his clock: 9:25. An hour late. He hadn't expect to be gone so long. He let himself into the darkened kitchen and poured himself a glass of orange juice before joining his dad in front of the TV. Plopping down on the couch, he pretended not to notice the

23

blazing look directed his way from the brown leather La-Z-Boy.

"Trevor, I'm disappointed," his father snapped. "You think you're so smart, and that your mom and I are so stupid. You think I wasn't 17 once? I know what you did this afternoon by the smell on your clothes."

"Dad, I can explain, if you'll stop jumping to conclusions," Trevor said defensively. "I'll admit that some of the guys at James's house were drinking and smoking dope, but I wasn't one of them. I've worked too hard to waste it on that junk."

"Ever heard about being guilty by association?" his dad shot back.

"Hey, hey! Where's all this coming from? Did you have one of your drug cops swing by James's place or something?" Trevor challenged. "Because if you did, that's really stupid."

"You're absolutely right I did!" his father yelled. "What did you think I'd do? You left this house to hang with a guy who I've heard is no good. Did you think I *wasn't* going to have one of my guys tail you?" he demanded, gesturing wildly. "Your mother was worried— but this isn't about your mom and me, Trevor. It's about you. It just so happens that James's house is under surveillance. We've been tracking him for the past couple months, following up on tips that he's been dealing drugs to Lincoln Southeast students."

"So are you going to haul me in, or what?" Trevor spat out. "Do you have me on tape smoking or drinking anything? . . . I didn't think so. I'm not interested in that stuff. I was just chillin' with the guys and some of my fans."

Duaine gave Trevor a sideways look. "OK. I want to make this really clear," he said quietly.

Upstairs Ardyce put down her book to hear better what Duaine was saying to their only child.

"I've got surveillance on many of your friends' houses. You need to watch yourself. I know what you're doing more than you think, so I better not hear about you at a drug party anytime soon, where girls are wearing only their underwear."

"Whatever!" Trevor huffed. "It's clear you believe your paid snoops more than you believe me." He heaved himself off the couch. "I'm going up to my room to study."

"Listen carefully, son. If I catch you at another party like this I'll have them haul you in. You'll see how cool it is to spend a night in jail. It's no pot party with chicks in bras, I can tell you that much."

Trevor scowled darkly and went upstairs. He gave his bedroom door a hefty shove, making sure it shut good and tight. He took a few running steps and leaped onto his bed, closed his eyes, and tried to think.

"I did not see that coming," he breathed. "I wonder how many other parties Dad's sent his goons to that I didn't know about. No wonder the druggies make a point to get far away from me before they make a sale."

Slithering out of his shirt and throwing it across his eyes, Trevor decided he would pay more attention to where he went on the weekends, and whom he was with. He'd never let his dad know it, but this surveillance stuff really tripped him out.

Ardyce slipped silently into the room just as Duaine turned off the TV. "Why didn't you tell me you were following Trevor?" she asked quietly. "Don't you trust him? He's a good kid, and he loves you a lot. He's pushed himself too long and hard to waste it on drugs and girls. Why don't you give him the benefit of the doubt, as you do with other kids you catch in bad situations?"

"Benefit of the doubt? OK, I'll be honest with you. I didn't tell you all I knew about our son and his activities before he left today. I didn't tell you because I didn't want you getting too worried." He looked at her for a long moment. "But at the same time, Trevor's one of the most popular kids at school, so I have my guard up even more with him. I have to. My reputation rests on it. If Trevor's not careful, he'll lose all he's worked for, and I'm certainly not going to let that happen. Besides, he'll thank me later."

"Well, don't be so quick to pat yourself on the back, Duaine," Ardyce said stiffly. "What good will your so-called help be if you don't have a relationship with him anymore? He's not as bad as some of the kids you deal with. Trevor's very impressionable. And he values your opinion about him more than you realize."

Chapter 3

Trevor was very good at hiding his true thoughts and feelings. Even while he partied with the football team and threw a football around with his dad, he was thinking about whether he really wanted to play football his senior year at Lincoln Southeast High. He liked football a lot—maybe even more than baseball—and had collected football cards as a kid. But there was his future to think about . . .

Then one day while he and his dad were playing catch in the backyard, he said, "Dad, I'm not playing football this year. I think I need to put more time into my pitching. Baseball's my best chance to make a name for myself. Besides, I don't think I weigh enough to play football at the college level."

Having delivered this message all in one breath, Trevor inhaled loudly and looked toward his dad to gauge his reaction. Duaine had been a star running back in high school, and Trevor was pretty sure it would disappoint him to hear that his only son wouldn't make him proud in football.

Duaine tucked the football under his arm and stared without expression at Trevor. "Son, I'm not that surprised by your decision," he finally said. "In fact, I think it's the best decision you could've made for your baseball career. As far as sports go, your pitching has always been what's made you special and better than everyone else."

He held his hand out for a shake, then pulled him a little closer. "I'm proud of you. You made a man's decision, one that many of your friends and people in this community are going to criticize. But they're not you. They don't know your struggles and your aspirations. Expect some of your football teammates and girl groupies to cuss you out, though," he added with a laugh.

As they walked to the house Duaine reached out and lightly rubbed his son's left shoulder blade. "You've got a gift with that throwing arm," he mused. "Your mom and I will always support you when it comes to baseball."

Trevor smiled. Though he'd never get all mushy about it, he really did appreciate the support of his parents. He knew that not many of his friends had parents who were as devoted as his were. "Listen, Dad, I'm going to need a little extra help improving my pitching. I need to throw the ball around daily—even in bad weather—to build up my stamina."

"I'd be happy to work with you," his dad responded. "Just don't kill me in the process."

Summer football practice was set to begin in two weeks. Trevor knew he needed to tell Coach Mike Capron that he wasn't going to be the starting quarterback, but he decided not to say anything until after he'd lifted weights one more time, because he figured the coach would be angry and might not allow him to work out in the weight room.

So after a good workout Trevor showered and got dressed, then tapped on the coach's open door. "Coach, can I talk to you? It's important."

"Sure." The coach had been watching a video of Southeast's first opponent, Lincoln Pius. He hit pause on the remote and turned. "Whatcha need, Bullock?"

"Well, I know our first game is just three weeks away, but . . ." Trevor's voice trailed off.

Coach Capron chuckled. "But you're having a hard time keeping all the plays straight? Do ya keep getting them confused with all the girls' phone numbers you've got stored in that pretty head of yours?" he asked with a smirk.

"No, Coach, it's nothing like that. It's, well, I'm not going to play football this year," Trevor blurted. "I'm sorry it's late notice and all, but my heart just isn't in it. I'm afraid I'll get my pitching arm hurt, and—"

Coach Capron interrupted. "Look, I understand, Trevor." But his tone held little understanding. "You're an arrogant, self-centered punk!" His eyes were dark with anger. "You carry on with me and the guys like you're with us 100 percent, then come by here with three weeks to spare and say, 'Oh, by the way, I've changed my mind.'"

Trevor leaned casually against the wall and looked at Coach Capron with a half-raised eyebrow.

"Bullock, I hate the way everything is all about you. You're so certain the world revolves around you that you even came in here to get one last round in on the weights before you told me. You think I didn't notice? You know, we're probably better off without you. I'll tell the guys. Now get out of here!"

Standing up straight, Trevor said, "Thanks for telling the guys. I don't want them to hate me. And I do want you to know that I had a hard time making this decision. It's just that I think I should work on my pitching. I want to get noticed by some college scouts in the spring."

Capron gave him a stony look. "You made your decision. I don't like it, and I don't have to. Now I mean it: get out! I've got a football *team* to worry about, and I don't need any more of your me-first attitude hanging around my office. It's obvious you aren't a team player, and I'm done with you."

The next day Trevor stopped by Seth's house. "Coach said you're quitting on us," Seth said from where he sprawled on the couch watching *Dazed and Confused* for the umpteenth time. The movie depicting a group of bored Texas high schoolers who play football and smoke weed always seemed to be running in the background whenever any of the Southeast football players were together. "I can't believe you waited this long to tell anybody you were quitting. How long have you been thinking about it?"

Trevor shrugged. "All summer."

Seth stared challengingly at him.

Trevor dropped his eyes. "What? You think this was an easy decision for me? I know everybody around school is going to be trying to get in my face about it. But I've made up my mind that this is what's best for my future. My future is in baseball. Look, if you pitched like me you'd probably do the same thing." Trevor was a little irritated that nobody seemed to see things his way.

"No, that's where you're wrong." Seth took a sip of his Coke in an effort to keep his temper in check. "Dude, I'm not like you. Nobody's like you. You're selfish. You think of yourself before anybody else. But hey, don't get me wrong—that's who you are. That's what makes you such a maddeningly good athlete and chick magnet. You've got the attitude, and you don't care if people hate you."

Seth reached out and pushed Trevor's head back with the palm of his hand. "I hate your guts, Trevor," he muttered. "And here I am asking you to come on over to my house because I just like you so much." He shook his head. Not only was Trevor the best quarterback Seth had ever worked with, but hanging out with him meant he got to hang out with the pretty girls too. Right now, though, he was sick of Trevor's attitude and sick of always being in his shadow. "Look, I'm just going to miss your intensity in the huddle, OK?"

"Hey, man, I'm going to miss you, too," Trevor said. "But I've still got your back at parties. I'm coming to the one on Friday at Mack's place, so I'll see you there."

"Are you crazy?" Seth sputtered, nearly choking on his Coke. "You're actually planning on coming to a football party after leaving us with that idiot junior jerk Rich Carroll as our starting quarterback?"

Trevor laughed and grabbed a loaded cheese nacho chip from the coffee table. "Sure I'm coming! Nobody's going to get too crazy. I'll bring some hot chicks with me—some young ones who are eager to please. That will mellow everybody out."

Seth gave him a sideways look and shook his head. Trevor wasn't even sorry for leaving the team high and dry. And the frustrating thing was that he was probably right—most likely he'd be able to smooth everything over with a few cute little freshman girls. How aggravating!

☆ ☆ ☆

"So what are you going to do with all your spare time?" Luke asked. He was a tight end from the football team. He slipped into the booth across from Trevor at Dairy Queen and started helping himself to Trevor's Blizzard. All week long people had been coming up to Trevor and asking the same sort of questions.

Pulling his Blizzard back, Trevor replied, "What do you think I'm going to do with it? I'm going to work on my pitching more. I need more than just the three pitches I have now."

"Hey, that's cool, man," Luke grinned. "You'll probably make it to the majors in spite of the fact that you drink too much beer. I'm just jealous, that's all. You're the only person I know who can plow everybody else over in sports while still partying like an idiot, plus have any girl you want."

"Give me a break!" Trevor laughed, but he was pleased. "You know I'm just a fool like everybody else. I mean, I love my parents. Who admits to that? My dad's kind of intense, but I'd do anything for him. In fact, that's what motivates me. My dad, pitching in the majors—and girls."

Luke gave Trevor his half grin again and got up to leave. "Fool" was one word he'd never use to describe Trevor, but it was obvious that Trevor loved all the attention he was getting from quitting the football team, and Luke wasn't going to play into that any longer.

☆ ☆ ☆

Trevor could hear the hip-hop music booming from two blocks away, shaking the windows at the party that was just picking up steam at Kayla's house this warm Friday night in early September. Aaron, Nate, and Trevor got out of the car and headed for the front door. About 70 people milled about in and around the house that backed up against a wooded area at the end of a long street. What a great place for a party! The few neighbors who might have been bothered by the noise were away for the weekend.

Once in the house Trevor instantly attracted the attention of a couple girls. Amy Swartz was a little short, but Trevor had known her since kindergarten and had to admit she had blossomed into a pretty shapely girl. Tonight her dark auburn hair was down and curled around her face. Holding a can of Miller Lite in her hand, she approached Trevor and swayed slightly into him. "I'm glad you're here!" she gushed as she tried to rebalance herself against his shoulder.

"Yeah, it's great to see you, Trevor!" Jennifer Bailey added, approaching him on the other side. She had a can of Miller Lite, too, and her face was slightly flushed. "You're the life of the party, Trevor. I want to hang with you more than anybody else." Then with a silly giggle she fell against the wall for support.

Putting an arm around each girl, Trevor said, "Well, it's nice to see you ladies, too! Give me a swig from each of your beers. I'm ready to get hammered with you two."

"Trevor, you can have the whole can as far as I'm concerned," Amy babbled effusively.

Across the room Aaron signaled Trevor that he was leaving. Nate gave Trevor a goofy face and followed after Aaron. Nate never drank at parties, and Aaron didn't stay long enough to know he'd come. They both kept an eye out for Trevor, though. *He* was the party animal.

Turning back to the girls, Trevor asked, "Do either of you have any weed? It's been a pretty stressful week, and I want to get stoned."

"No, Trevor," Amy said. "Remember? I don't smoke dope."

"Me neither," Jennifer added. "But I saw Jeff and Gunner with a bowl out by the pool. I'm sure they'd let you share."

Trevor smiled as he stepped away. "You girls stay right here, and I'll be back. Then the three of us can hang out."

Winding his way through the crowd of students in varying degrees of drunkenness and agitation, Trevor finally found Jeff and Gunner sitting next to the hot tub, holding a smoldering bowl between them. "Hey, guys, I heard you could hook me up with some of what you've got."

"Sure, I got some chronic," Gunner sniffed. "But I'm not sure I wanna share since you quit on the team, Pretty Boy."

"Don't call me Pretty Boy!" Trevor shot back irritably. "And get over yourself already. I'm not in the mood to take your lip about quitting football." Were they ever going to leave him alone about it? "Look, are you going to give me a round with that bowl, or not?"

"Dude, chill out," Gunner muttered. "I'll let you have your stupid—"

Suddenly a shout rang out: "COPS! COPS! COPS!"

For a split second the three boys froze. A wave of panic washed across Gunner's face as a pair of muscular undercover drug enforcement officers barreled into the yard, scattering students in all directions. Gunner and Jeff ran one way, and Trevor ran another. He scaled the fence and ran along the back side of the neighbors' yards, sprinting so hard he felt as if his heart were going to jump right out of his chest. He came to a side street and glanced over his shoulder. One of the officers was still pursuing him.

As Trevor uttered an expletive under his breath, his thoughts began to churn. *I am not going to go down like this! I have worked too hard at keeping this from my dad. This is not going to blow up over me getting caught trying to share a bowl. I didn't even get any!* Forcing his legs to move even faster, he vowed, "I am *not* going to get snagged!"

Then he tripped and fell hard over a rain gutter and knocked the wind out of himself. Inhaling sharply, he noticed some bushes off to the side and crawled under one. He grasped the base of one bush and held on tight, not even feeling the rough pieces of bark digging into his palms. His pulse pounded in his head, and his chest burned. He forced himself to sit absolutely still, breathing slowly and quietly through his nose. Sweat dripped down his forehead and into his eyes as he squinted through the branches at the street in front of him. "O God, please don't let me get caught!"

The cop rounded the corner and slowed to a jog before stopping right in front of Trevor. He was lean and muscular with a blond buzz cut. He looked like a Navy Seal, and he wanted to find Trevor. With his hands on his waist he glanced around. Trevor could hear his heavy breathing in the sultry night air. Scanning the rooftops and trees carefully, the cop slowly and deliberately began walking backward to see if he'd missed something.

"Murph? You there?" the officer's radio crackled through the silence. "I've cornered the two punks I was chasing, but I need your help. Get over here, pronto! One of these guys is big, and he looks like he wants to challenge me."

"Hey, Smitty," Murph replied, "I'm on my way. What's your 20?" He began running again.

Trevor released a long, nervous sigh of relief. His mouth was parched, and his back ached. He was about to stretch out a little bit when he heard several sirens. He could see the lights and hear the shouts as a half dozen Lincoln Police Department squad cars arrived on the chaotic scene.

Pulling his legs back up to his chest, Trevor hunkered down again. He was afraid to come out of his hiding spot—it wasn't worth the risk of being brought into jail and humiliated by his dad's subordinates. *What was I thinking?* he admonished himself. *How could I let this happen? I don't want to lose my good name over some dope. I am such an idiot,* suuuuch *an idiot!*

Swallowing hard, he promised himself, *This will not happen again.*

The adrenaline had drained from his veins, replaced by a feeling of utter fatigue. He laid his head on his knees and drifted off to sleep.

A half hour later Trevor's slumber was shattered by the sound of a nearby car alarm. Glancing around, he could see that the officers were gone. His watch read 9:49. Cautiously he stretched out his legs, then ducked out from under the bush and straightened up. Walking stiffly along the fence line, he headed toward home, avoiding the sidewalk. The night air had become cool, and he was shivering.

When he was four houses away he checked his watch again: 9:53. He surveyed the damage to his clothes. Just a little dirt spot on his knees. He'd find some excuse for that if his mom noticed. His dad got off work at 10:00, and he wanted to be home before his dad arrived—and before his mom began to wonder about him.

Walking briskly, he tucked in his shirt and zipped up his jacket. He ran his fingers through his sweaty, tousled hair, and pulled his house key from his pocket. As he unlocked the door he could see his mom sitting on the living room couch, reading her Bible.

"Hey, Mom!" he called cheerfully. Staying in the shadows of the kitchen cabinets, he slipped down the hall to the bathroom to inspect himself in the mirror. Then he walked back to the kitchen to get a drink of water.

"Did you have a good time at Kayla's?" Ardyce asked. "I heard sirens coming from that direction. Did the party get broken up? Where have you been this whole time?"

"Oh, yeah, I went to Aaron's for a while after," Trevor said. "Listen, I'm going to take a shower and then go to bed. It's been a long week."

"That's fine," Ardyce called after him. "Remember, we have church tomorrow, and I expect you to be ready for Sabbath school by 9:05. You got it?"

"Yeah, yeah. I'll see you in the morning."

He let the hot water pour over his back, relaxing all the knots. Turning to face the showerhead, he leaned heavily against the wall. He'd been lucky tonight. More than anything else he was relieved that he'd avoided embarrassment in front of his dad. He knew he'd have been royally chewed out if the narcs had hauled him in.

33

Chapter 4

Trevor awoke to a loud thumping on his door. Raising his head sleepily, he turned to the clock and stared at the numbers until they came into focus: 7:47. He let his head drop back on the pillow. A hair dryer kicked on across the hall in his parents' room. The sound of water rushing through the pipes indicated someone was taking a shower.

Then it dawned on him—it was Sabbath. Maybe if he pretended to be totally dead asleep he could avoid church. As a child Trevor had gone to church regularly with his mother, but as he got older church had become a bore. The truth was that although Trevor's mom had been an Adventist her whole life, his dad had never been one. True, Duaine Bullock had joined his wife at church during Trevor's early years, but, like his son, his attendance had become more sporadic the past several years. This Sabbath, though, they had both promised to go with her, and Trevor knew he was going to have to keep his word.

A loud, persistent knock interrupted Trevor's thoughts; then his mother's head peeked around the door. "All right, Trevor," she said sternly. "You promised. Get up!" She swept into the room and opened the blinds, letting in a burst of light. "I know you were out partying last night and you probably don't feel like moving this morning, but we're leaving in less than an hour, and I expect you to be ready."

"OK, OK, OK," Trevor answered groggily, pushing his legs out from under the covers and stumbling out of bed. "Did you leave me any hot water?"

"Well, I guess you'll find out soon enough," his mom laughed.

"There should be enough for at least a two-minute shower," his dad yelled as he tugged down on his tie.

"That's not funny, Dad," Trevor shouted back. "You know how I depend on a shower to wake up."

"You took one last night, didn't you?" his dad asked as he walked into the hallway, dressed for church. "You'll be fine without one—just wet your hair. No one will know the difference. Plus, you'll be downstairs that much faster to get some grub in ya."

Trevor did a quick mental replay of last night's events, then agreed. "You're right; I did shower last night. I guess I will just wet my hair."

Thirty minutes later he dashed into the kitchen, freshly shaved and looking dapper as always in a suit. Downing a glass of orange juice, he said, "Let's go! I'll eat in the car." He grabbed a banana and one of his favorite vanilla cream long-john doughnuts from Conroy's Bakery, and headed toward the door.

"Good!" his mother approved. "We'll be on time for church for the first time in—I don't know how long."

"Not to be disrespectful or anything, but why do people have to go to church every week?" Trevor complained. "I mean, why can't a person go only every now and then? Let's be honest: most of the time when I do go I'm bored out of my mind. The only thing that's good about church is seeing all the girls dressed up nice. I love seeing them—well, some of them anyway."

Rolling her eyes, Ardyce interrupted him. "This is Sabbath, Trevor. What has gotten into you lately? All you talk about is girls and baseball." With a frustrated sigh she added, "You go to church to learn more about God and to build a relationship with Him. You're not there to check out the girls."

"Honey, what do you expect?" Duaine interjected as they got into the car together. "When I was his age, all I thought about were girls too."

Ardyce didn't hide her annoyance. "Really now, it's Sabbath, you two. Can we please change the subject?"

"OK; sorry," the two chastised Bullocks muttered.

Ardyce was just barely beginning to create a feeling of Sabbath rest and joy in her heart when Duaine broke the silence. "Hey, Trevor, tell me more about Kayla's party last night."

Hoping he sounded nonchalant, Trevor said, "It was an all-right party."

His dad caught his eye in the rearview mirror. "Where were you when our officers broke up the party? Did you see the bust?"

Searching his mind for a quick way out of this conversation, Trevor admitted, "I saw it all. It was pretty intense. The cops just came out of nowhere on those guys."

"Yeah, we got a couple of them. There was a third kid, but that lucky punk got away." He looked at Trevor steadily. "He won't be so fortunate next time."

The silence was thick. In a minute his dad continued, "The kids in your class sure have an appetite for drugs. Those friends of yours really keep us busy. It surprises me how many athletes use that junk. Don't get me wrong. We weren't perfect when I was a kid, but I never would have done anything to ruin my chances as an athlete."

"Yeah, you're right; it's kind of crazy, Dad." He hoped his dad was finished with this subject. And seeing the way his mother was slumped against her side of the car, Trevor was pretty sure this wasn't the change of subject she'd been hoping for either.

But Duaine wasn't finished. "Trevor, I know I give you advice all the time, and I've probably said this to you before, but be careful who you hang with." He paused to make sure Trevor was listening. "Nothing will end your dreams of major league baseball faster than hanging out with some stupid drug dealer. You hear me? You know what I'm saying?"

"Oh, I know exactly what you're saying, Dad. Don't worry about me. I'm listening to what you say, and I know you're right."

Trevor was thankful to see that they were arriving at the church. He really hoped he'd been convincing. He hoped his dad would drop the subject. Besides, after spending all that time under a bush he was truly feeling receptive to his father's admonitions.

Later that afternoon Trevor admitted, "Mom, I'm so bored in Sabbath school. All I do is sit there with my head down and check out everybody else's shoes."

Ardyce knew it was true. She knew that because Trevor didn't go to College View Academy as most of the other kids in the class did, he felt like an outsider. He didn't respond to questions in class or offer any input at all. It was obvious for anybody to see that he read his *Insight*

magazine during church and often fell asleep. So did his dad.

Ardyce gave him a halfhearted smile. "I do know it's hard to feel as if you don't belong," she began, choosing her words carefully. "But this stuff that puts you and your dad to sleep could really make your life better—if you listened to it and applied it. I pray for you every day, Trevor. I pray that someday your life will reflect Jesus in spite of this sex-crazed world you're growing up in."

Hoping to make his mom feel better, Trevor said, "I listen, Mom. Sometimes. But most of the time I find this stuff so boring and irrelevant. I mean, most of this stuff happened so long ago it's beyond comprehension. I just can't identify with most of it. It would be cool if there were some Bible stories about sports."

Ardyce sighed. "Trevor, perhaps if you were open-minded enough you could see that God helped David to be a pretty fantastic pitcher. He slew Goliath with just a few smooth stones."

☆ ☆ ☆

The next months passed quickly as Trevor prepped for his senior baseball season. Every day he practiced throwing with his dad. He lifted weights, and ran five times a week. But despite all his efforts to make his senior season a memorable one, he continued to live life foolishly off the field. For one thing, he had two girlfriends, one at Southeast High and one at a rival school. Since Lincoln Southeast High School had an enrollment of 1,852 students, 583 in Trevor's class alone, the unwitting girls didn't catch on to Trevor's two-timing ways for a while.

Besides trying to stay out of girl trouble, Trevor continued to drink and sometimes smoke marijuana on the weekends. After trying drugs the year before out of "curiosity," he had begun to like it and had become a bit too casual about it.

"Hey, you're looking kind of tired," Trevor yelled over the noise of the car radio. He and Seth were cruising around Lincoln in Trevor's car. "Let me take you home."

"This weed I got from James is stronger than he usually sells us," Seth speculated after taking a drag from his pipe. "It's making me a lot more drowsy and hungry."

"This stuff is no different than usual," Trevor laughed, picking up the pipe to try some for himself. "You're just more tired than you realize. You've been hanging out too much with Lacey and all her easy friends."

As they turned the corner, the boys spotted a police car, its blue and red patrol lights flickering frantically behind a car that had been pulled over. Trevor causally snuffed out the pipe and set it in his ashtray. "Nothing like a Friday n ight to bring out Lincoln's red and blue squad," he commented sarcastically.

"Is your dad working tonight?" Seth asked.

"No, I think he's already home," Trevor replied as he pulled into Seth's driveway. "Sometimes he works on Friday nights, but most times he tries to come home early to make my mom happy. It's her Sabbath." Not wanting to have to explain the finer details of Adventism to Seth, he said, "Well, have a good night," and motioned for Seth to get out of the car.

Stepping into his darkened house, Trevor headed for the fridge to see if there were any leftovers from supper. He was hungry, and he'd also discovered that eating a lot made his parents worry less about him. If he got good grades and did well in sports, he could get by with just about anything. And if he kept a pretty girlfriend and maintained a hearty appetite, nobody ever asked any questions.

Ardyce opened her bedroom door and came down the hall. "Is that you, Trevor?" she called.

"Yeah, it's me, Mom."

She stopped midstep. "You smell like marijuana."

"Well, I was just at a party where people were smoking dope," Trevor replied quickly. "I didn't do anything, but it's hard not to get the smell in your clothes. Don't worry—I'm too good of an athlete to mess with that junk."

Ardyce gave him a long look. "You really should get to bed. I'll see you in the morning."

The next morning Trevor heard his dad quietly enter his room. He rolled over and buried his head deeper into his pillow. Trevor knew his dad was just going to move his car so he could get out of the driveway and go to work.

But two minutes later Trevor felt as if a bomb had exploded in his head. His dad was pounding on his door. Bolting out of bed on pure adrenaline, Trevor flung open the door and exclaimed, "What are you doing, Dad?"

Wordlessly Duaine held up the pot pipe that Seth had left in the car. Trevor felt all his blood drain into his toes. His dad was breathing in heavy bursts, and Trevor could see angry (or was it sad?) tears pooling in his father's eyes. Then he abruptly turned and walked back down the hall. Nobody had said anything, but Trevor was suddenly aware that his heart was pounding and his mouth was as dry as the desert.

Duaine Bullock drove to work in an angry fog. How could Trevor have lied and deceived him like this? And why had he been so trusting? He'd seen the signs. He'd noticed the leaves that had fallen inside the basement window when Trevor sneaked out. He'd heard the other officers talk about seeing Trevor at parties. They said that Trevor was cocky and walked right up to them, challenging them. "My dad will believe me before he'll believe you, so go ahead and talk bad about me to him. He'll fire you for it."

Whom was he kidding? He'd seen Trevor with his own eyes on the surveillance cameras. He climbed out of his car at the station and walked inside. He startled everybody when he barked, "Anybody here *not* know what my son looks like?"

The officers silently shook their heads and stared at him.

"Anybody here *not* know what kind of car my son drives?"

Again they shook their heads. Everybody knew Trevor.

"All right, then. There's no playing favorites here. You keep an eye on him. If you catch him drag racing, bring him in. Doing dope? Bring him in. Drinking? Bring him in. Any questions?"

There were none.

"And one more thing. I want that James Bishop kid indicted. *Now!*"

At home that night Trevor avoided his dad. Never in his life had he seen his dad with anything close to tears in his eyes. When Duaine called Trevor to come out of his room, he shuffled into the kitchen, knowing he was going to have to face his father.

"Look, I'm sorry, Dad—"

Duaine cut him off. "I'm so angry I'm half tempted to haul you in myself and lock you up. But I won't. You need to know that you're grounded for the next month until baseball season starts. I don't care that you're missing a ski trip to Colorado. You're staying right here in this house. Do you understand?"

"Yes, Dad," Trevor said weakly.

"I'm sick of you thinking you're invincible because I'm the narc captain." Duaine was getting revved up. "And we've got enough to arrest James Bishop, so I hope that will slow you down."

Trevor nodded. He was terrified to hear about James, but he hoped it didn't show.

"We've been following James for four years now," Duaine continued. "You better watch out who you hang with. These habits are going to get you into trouble."

Chapter 5

He was heading into the first game of his senior year, and Trevor knew there would be college scouts at the game. He was actually looking forward to it. He liked it when reporters wanted to talk with him. He liked the pressure of high expectations from the crowd. And he loved trying to impress the girls. He had played baseball for 13 years, and he was ready to be a star. He knew he could put the ball wherever he wanted it to go. He knew he could have any girl he wanted. The world was his, and he planned on taking it.

But the game had a shaky start. He walked the first batter, then allowed a double down the line into right field. After only two batters Millard South had runners on second and third. Both batters had worked full counts. He was sure he was throwing strikes, but the ump was calling them balls.

"C'mon, Blue!" Ardyce yelled from the stands after each ball. It sounded as if she was already getting hoarse.

The "missed" calls infuriated Trevor. Nate took off his catcher's mask and jogged out to the mound. "Dude, don't let this ump get the best of you," he instructed. "I'm sure he's heard a lot about you and wants to see what you're made of. He's challenging you. So are you up for the challenge, or are you just going to sulk and throw this game away?" As he turned to leave he said, "Get your head in the game and kick some butt."

Stepping off the mound, Trevor decided to do exactly what his cousin had suggested: get his head in gear. He scanned the crowd and grinned at a pair of girls who were flirting with him. They were seated directly behind three guys who were holding radar guns and carrying notebooks. Duaine, in his usual spot near the first base line, whistled and shouted, "Focus, Trevor! Be mentally tough. This is your game."

As he got back on the mound he heard Coach McLaughlin call from the dugout, "Relax, T-Bull. Show 'em what you got!"

Trevor was looking in for the sign from Nate when the umpire raised his hands signaling a time-out. The left-handed batter, Jeremy Lyons, had stepped out of the batter's box.

Hoping that he had thrown Trevor out of his newly strengthened focus, Lyons cracked, "Hey, Mr. Preseason All-district! You think I'm gonna let you get comfortable out there? I can't wait to see you fall flat on your pretty-boy face!"

"You talking to me?" Trevor yelled, stepping off the mound and walking toward home plate. "Don't think that I won't make you and all your teammates pay for the stupid things you say. Your mouth won't be able to back you up."

"Hey, pal, you don't want to upset my cousin," Nate interjected from his crouch position behind the plate. "It doesn't take that much to get him going. He also pitches better when he's mad, and I think you just pushed his button. I guess you and the rest of your sorry teammates can forget about impressing anybody today now that you've gotten Trevor worked up."

"Hey, fat boy, was I talking to you?" Lyons shot back. He adjusted his batting helmet and stepped back in the batter's box. "You just tell your hotheaded, pretty-boy cousin to give me his best pitch, and we'll see who's talking then."

Nate signaled a slider. Trevor shook it off. Nate scowled and sent the signal again. Trevor raised his eyebrow and shook it off again. "He's so stupid," Nate muttered under his breath to Lyons. "It never matters how many times I tell him not to shake me off, he still does it. So you listening? He's gonna throw a sinker."

Lyons couldn't believe what he was hearing, but he held up on the pitch and, sure enough, the ball came in straight and then dropped into the dirt for a ball.

Feeling empowered by this strange camaraderie with Nate, Lyons laughed and said, "Tell him to give me his overhyped heater. I can't wait to club a homer off his sorry pitch."

Nate signaled a four-seam fastball. Trevor nodded his head forward and dealt the pitch down the middle of the plate. Lyons swung late.

Strike one. Lyons stepped out of the batter's box and readjusted his batting helmet.

"He's better than you thought, isn't he?" Nate teased.

Lyons ignored him.

"Well, *I'm* enjoying this," Nate chortled, and sent Trevor the sign for a rising fastball. Trevor nodded and rocked into his quick motion. He released an inside fastball that tailed up. Lyons swung and missed.

With the count at one and two the home crowd roared. And Trevor grinned. Now he was having fun too.

"We're having some good times," Nate mocked Lyons. "I'm really enjoying this. Your bat can't keep up with your mouth."

Lyons ignored Nate and sent Trevor a withering look.

"So, now you can't talk smack, huh?" Nate ribbed. "You're one strike away from choking. I wish all hitters were cocky fools like you."

Nate signaled another sinker. Trevor shook off the sign.

"Well, here we go again," Nate snapped to Lyons. "He's shaking me off. So I'll give you another chance to know what's coming, all right? Let's see if you can use the advantage to let everybody know you're not terrible!"

Rolling his eyes at the chatty catcher, Lyons responded with a clipped "So what's it gonna be?"

"Here comes a changeup. It's gonna be *slow!* You got it?" Nate was clearly in jovial spirits.

Trevor delivered. Lyons almost swung, but stopped himself right before his bat crossed the plate. Now the count was two and two.

"You know, Lyons, I'm really getting tired of you," Nate quipped. "Most batters don't last as long as you have. And you're not even any good. I say we get you out of here."

"Suit yourself, fat boy," Lyons jeered as he tipped his batting helmet on tighter.

"Oh, silent guy speaks again," Nate mocked. "OK, here comes a curveball. You ready?"

He sent the sign, and Trevor agreed. The pitch sailed to the outside of the plate.

Stepping in, Lyons barely reached it. The ball dribbled just to the left of Trevor as the runner on third took off for home. Trevor picked up the ball and tossed it to Nate for the first out, but Lyons was safe on first. And they had another runner on third.

The crowd cheered.

Nate threw Trevor the ball and jogged to the mound.

"You were telling Lyons what I was gonna throw, weren't you?" Trevor accused, gesturing wildly. "You're such an idiot! You make me so mad!"

"Good." Nate was giggling. "You pitch so much better when you're mad."

"You're out of your mind!" Trevor's voice cracked into the falsetto range.

"Well, this will teach you not to wave me off." Nate shook his finger in front of Trevor's face in playful reproach. "I know what's best for you. Just remember the kisses you'll get from those girls behind the radar guys if you pitch well." He scampered back behind the plate. He nodded knowingly to the umpire. "I think he wants to kill me. But he's got his little strut back, and you watch: he'll be throwing strikes now."

The ump gave a humorless grunt. This catcher was unbelievable. What a mouthy kid.

Trevor accepted Nate's next signal, and the next batter hit a high infield popup for an easy out. Trying not to be too obvious, Trevor glanced at the girls. He hoped they were digging him. Just one more out, and he'd have this inning in the bag.

Millard South's next batter was a free-swinger named Johnny Jackson. Nate signaled for another sinker. Trevor delivered, and Jackson fouled down the third baseline for a strike. Nate asked for the same pitch again, and Trevor agreed. This time Jackson missed entirely. Strike two.

Jackson stepped out of the batter's box to clear his head. This Bullock guy was frustrating. Who did he think he was, pitching in the dirt like that?

Trevor waited patiently for Jackson to collect himself. Then he threw the ball in the dirt again, this time hard on the inside. Jackson had to dance out of the way to avoid getting hit. One ball and two strikes.

Trevor was frustrated. He hadn't intended for the ball to go quite so far inside, and it bothered him that his accuracy had faltered. He wasn't going to take another signal from Nate for a slider; he didn't care what his crazy cousin thought was good for him. That last pitch was a disaster.

"Is he going to throw me anything to hit, or what?" Jackson asked Nate. "I thought your pitcher was supposed to be so amazing. Right now, all he's throwing is junk out of the zone. He hasn't shown me much at all."

Nate didn't answer. This was the perfect time for Trevor to send one more ball into the dirt. He signaled, and Trevor waved him off. "Oh, no, you don't!" Nate muttered. That Trevor was so irritatingly arrogant. "Well, all right, then," he said to no one in particular. "Show me your fastball off the plate." Signaling to Trevor for the fastball, Nate spoke evenly and clearly: "Are you listening, Jackson? You're going to get that fastball you've been hungry for."

Trevor delivered the pitch. Jackson was ready. He tattooed the ball deep to left field. Eric Strickland had come in and now had to dive in order to snag the ball with the tip of his glove. The ball hit the ground hard and popped out of his glove. Both Millard South runners scored, and Jackson reached second with a stand-up double.

The Lincoln Southeast crowd became eerily quiet. Their star pitcher had just allowed two runs in the first inning. Trevor kicked up dirt on the mound and fumed. "I can't believe this!"

"Oh, calm down, you big baby," Nate cajoled as he ran out halfway to the mound to give Trevor a new ball. "It's only the first inning. And it's only two runs. We've got seven innings to beat these guys up. Have you forgotten who *their* pitcher is? We knocked him around pretty good last year. So just relax and let Nate here tell you what to pitch. My pitches get you kisses."

"OK, you're right. It's still early," Trevor agreed. "Now go back to where you belong!"

He was still irritated. He didn't want to depend on the hitters to make up the runs off Millard's less-than-stellar pitcher. He wanted to be the star himself. Looking toward the first baseline, he saw his dad pointing toward his forehead. "Keep your head," he was saying.

Trevor closed his eyes and drew in a long breath. Turning to face the next batter, he struck him out—one, two, three—to get the final out. He walked slowly back to the dugout. He didn't like it when outfielders dropped the ball, and he intended to make Eric give him an answer about it.

Eric saw Trevor waiting for him and grinned sheepishly. "Hey, T-Bull, I know you're not happy about that, but the ball just came out when I hit the ground, OK? Don't sweat it. We'll still beat these guys."

"I know, but I just wish—"

Coach McLaughlin clamped his hand on Trevor's shoulder. "Eric gave it his best," he said firmly. "This is the first game of the season, and we have a few kinks to work out." Turning Trevor to face him, he said, "You need to remember that you have a good group of hitters and fielders behind you. You don't have to be perfect. So just relax, OK?"

"OK, Coach," Trevor mumbled. But he still wanted to be perfect.

Lincoln Southeast's first three batters reached base and quickly tied the game. The offensive outburst calmed Trevor down, and he ended the game having given up only those two runs in the first inning. Southeast won 6 to 2.

Trevor stepped off the field and scanned the stands for the girls he'd been admiring during the game. Seeing the slim, cute brunet with short curly hair, he walked casually over to her and said, "Hey, what's your name?"

"It's Erin. I'm a sophomore," she said, giving him a smile. "I've heard a lot about you and that Aaron Madsen guy, and I just wanted to see if you were as good as everyone says."

"Well, what do you think? Am I?" Trevor asked, taking off his hat and wiping off his sweaty forehead with his arm.

"You're pretty good, but you're pretty cocky, too!" she said with a laugh.

Trevor produced his most charming smile. "Oh, that's just part of my game. It's what I do on the field. But really, if you'd get to know me off the field you'd think I was pretty mellow."

"So who's your new friend, Trevor?" Ardyce had come out the stands and was waiting for him to finish up and get ready to go.

"This is Erin," Trevor said, turning his back slightly to indicate he really wanted his mom to leave him alone. "I just met her. She was just telling me I'm too cocky."

"Oh, Erin, don't you know? It's the cocky ones who are the biggest babies. They get their feelings hurt really easy. You might not want to be too honest with a cocky boy," Ardyce advised. Then smiling, she said, "Trevor, don't be too long. Your father and I have plans this evening, and we're having dinner right at 5:30."

"OK, Mom. I'll see you at home."

"I kind of need to get home myself," Erin announced.

"Well, wait!" Trevor stammered, "Can I have your phone number, or something? I want to get to know you better."

Erin smiled. "Look, Trevor, I just came here because I really like baseball. I'm not really looking to get to know you better."

Trevor was floored. What was this girl saying? "Well, could we talk again sometime?" he asked.

"I suppose we could," Erin conceded. "But I'm pretty busy. I'm usually in gymnastics practice at this time. Besides, you've had a lot of girlfriends."

"How do you know so much about me?" Trevor was feeling defensive now.

"Like I said, I like baseball. I've heard you're the best. So I wanted to see, that's all. Don't you know people talk? Don't you know that the other girls tell me you already have a girlfriend, maybe two?" She rolled her eyes and shook her head. "I'm not interested in being a part of that."

Trevor was stunned. This girl sure was blunt. He kind of liked it, even though she had a way of making his head spin that bothered him a lot.

Softening a little, Erin said, "I'll tell you what. I'll come to your next game, OK? And I'll cheer for you. Maybe I'll see you around." Then she turned and walked away. As Trevor stared after her in disbelief she called over her shoulder, "Have a good dinner with your parents. They seem pretty cool."

☆ ☆ ☆

"There was something different about that curly-haired beauty you were talking to," Ardyce commented as Trevor came through the door. "She seemed kind of young—but smarter than most of the girls you pick," she added dryly.

"What's that supposed to mean!" Trevor retorted. "Look, it wasn't any kind of big deal—she's just a girl I met two minutes before you came along."

Ardyce eyed him suspiciously. She could tell there had been something different about Trevor's exchange with Erin. It was true. Trevor was still a little rattled by it. It was as if Erin could see deep inside him, uncovering truths even he hadn't realized were there. It was unnerving—but in a good way. He shook his head.

Ardyce laughed. "That girl really struck a nerve with you!"

"Enough already, Mom! She's a cute girl I might like to get to know better, but that's it. I don't need another girlfriend."

"*Another* girlfriend?" Ardyce raised an eyebrow. "You have girlfriends other than Traci?"

Traci? Traci? Which girl was Traci? Trevor's head began to spin. Which girl did his mother think he was dating? He went to the fridge and poured himself a glass of orange juice while he collected himself. "Traci's my *main* girl," he said lightly. "It's just that sometimes there are other girls who think I like them more than I do, that's all. I don't need another one of those—another girlfriend wannabe."

"OK," Ardyce said, "because I didn't raise you to be a two-timer."

Duaine stuck his head around the corner and gave Trevor a knowing smile that clearly said, "I'm not going to help you out, buddy!"

Desperate to change the subject, Trevor said, "Hey, Dad, what did you think of the game?"

"Well," Duaine said, "I'd like to talk a little about your pitching. I saw a few things that concerned me. But I must say that I'm real proud of the way you pulled yourself together after the two runs in the first inning."

Trevor grinned. "Yeah, Dad; I'm figuring out how to relax and get my focus back. I just look at some pretty girls in the stands, and that helps me let go of the tension."

"Must all conversations lead to girls?" Ardyce snapped.

"Well, dear, since you asked, yes, they do." Duaine gave her a playful squeeze. "I always used to relax by looking at the girls too."

"Well, I just wish girls weren't such a motivating factor. All this talk seems so superficial—and demeaning. Girls are *people*. They're more than just bodies and smiles."

"I know, Mom. It's just that when I focus on an attractive girl in the stands, it makes my worries slip away and I pitch better," Trevor explained. Then hoping that he really *could* have a conversation that didn't lead to girls, he asked, "Hey, Dad, did you happen to find out where those scouts were from?"

Duaine laughed. "I tried not to come across like too much of a proud papa, but I did find out that one was from Nebraska and one was from Kearney. And I think the third one was actually from the New York Mets."

"Do you think they liked what they saw?"

"Trevor, I don't get into that with those guys. I don't think it's my place. We don't want to seem desperate. Your pitching needs to speak for itself," he added with finality.

"OK," Trevor said. It was all he *could* say. He wanted his pitching to speak for itself too, but he still wished he knew whether he was impressing anybody.

Chapter 6

Trevor's final season of high school baseball flew by. He pitched well enough to earn a $3,000 yearly athletic scholarship to the University of Nebraska at Kearney, which was about 90 minutes from his home in Lincoln. Kearney was the same school his father had attended before he joined the Marines and went to Vietnam.

The most attractive aspect of attending Kearney was the fact that he could be a starting pitcher right away. UNK, a Division II school, had an enrollment of only 8,000. The larger Division I schools often "redshirted" the high-ranking freshmen, meaning they spent a year on the bench learning the program's system. Trevor didn't want to spend a year on the bench, so the idea of being a star at a smaller school appealed to him. In 1995 Kearney's baseball record had been 18 wins and 25 losses. It would be fun to be the hero who made Kearney a winning team, especially as a freshman.

There was another draw to going to school in Kearney. For a small town of about 25,000 the party scene was lively. In fact, in 1994 *Playboy* magazine had voted Kearney one of the best party schools in the country. People said, "You can't spell drunk without UNK in it." Away from his parents and the prying eyes of his dad's fellow officers, Trevor partied hard, becoming more famous for his drinking and wild lifestyle than his pitching.

☆ ☆ ☆

"I want to get a tattoo," Trevor announced. He had called Aaron while he was home from Kearney over winter break

"What if you end up thinking it looks stupid after it's done—or after a couple years?" Aaron sounded skeptical. "Tattoos are kind of permanent. You know what I'm saying?"

"Yeah, I know what you're saying," Trevor replied. "But I could probably do something cool with my nickname, T-Bull. The artist can make it look like anything I want."

"What do you want?"

"Well, it might be fun to do a joker with his tongue sticking out. You know, a kind of in-your-face way of showing I'm the life of the party. And he could be wearing a hat that has baseballs on the ends instead of puffballs. And it could say 'T-Bull' on it."

"Aren't you even worried about what your dad will think?" Aaron asked.

Trevor snorted. "Who cares about my dad!"

"Well, remember how you wanted to get your ear pierced, but then you didn't after your dad said, 'Go right ahead, but it's gonna look really stupid when I tear it out!' Remember that?"

"Yeah, I remember; but I'm ready to live a little!" Trevor sounded defensive. "I'm on my own now; I'm in college. I don't need to worry about what my dad thinks anymore! Besides, most people don't even see a tattoo. Maybe my dad will never know."

A half hour later they walked into Lincoln's Hungry Eye Tattoo on 9th and O streets. Ralph Spangler, Sr., had run the business for about as long as the boys had been alive. The early-evening sun angled through the big front windows, casting shimmery blades of light across the floor, and the dominant smell was the unmistakable essence of old building mixed with soap and bleach.

"What can I do for you guys?" Ralph, Jr., inquired. His body, displaying an amazing array of tattooed images, was a walking billboard for his craft.

Pointing to Trevor, Aaron announced, "My friend here wants a tattoo, and I'm here to watch."

Stepping forward, Trevor asked, "Where do you want me?" It was apparent he was trying to impress Aaron.

"Well, what do you want to get?" the long-haired Ralph inquired.

"I'd like a joker put on my right shoulder blade. I want him sticking his tongue out," Trevor instructed confidently. "And on the top of

51

his hat I want baseballs instead of puffy balls. Then you have to put my nickname, 'T-Bull,' on the front of the hat."

Just having said it made Trevor more and more certain that he did indeed want to do this. His parents would probably freak, but so what? Once it was done they couldn't do anything about it. Knowing they couldn't change it sent a kind of power rush through Trevor.

"You sound like you've been thinking about this for a while. What colors do you want me to use?" Ralph asked.

"Do red and green," Trevor said, adding, "I suppose I have thought about this a lot. My dad is the captain of the narc unit here in Lincoln, and at first I guess I was just a little scared he'd come undone. But now I think it'll be really cool."

"You're nuts!" Aaron muttered under his breath.

Ralph nodded and smiled. "Sure; it'll be cool-looking. But while we're talking about your parents, let me see your license. if you're under 18 years old you can't do this without your parents' permission. I want to see proof."

Trevor pulled out his wallet and produced his driver's license, and Ralph directed him to a black leather chair.

Getting the tattoo did hurt a little, but Trevor tried to maintain a tough-guy grimace during the two-hour procedure. All the while Aaron kept up a running commentary of mock flubs and slipups by the tattoo guy. When it was finished, Trevor went to the mirror and peered over his shoulder at a professionally inked, 5" by 5", smart-aleck jester in the upper right section of his back. Then he paid Ralph, and the boys stepped out into the now-dark street.

Trevor knew his mom would be cooking something special for Friday night supper. He did like a home-cooked meal. . . . Maybe he'd even think about going to church in the morning. Turning to Aaron, he said, "Thanks. That was really fun. I think I'll head home to see my parents."

"Hey, dude, you're not wasting any time getting in their face with that thing, are you?" Aaron laughed and shook his head. "Well, good luck with that!"

☆ ☆ ☆

When they got home from church the next day, Trevor went to his room to change his clothes while his mom was making lunch. He craned his neck around so he could admire his tattoo in the mirror. The swelling had gone down some, and he thought it had turned out really well. He decided it was time to get his parents' reaction. They needed to see that he was making his own choices now.

So he left his shirt off and sauntered to the basement to watch TV with his dad. Duaine was focused on the screen when Trevor arrived, and saw nothing as his son sat down on the couch. When Ardyce came down the stairs to call them to lunch, Trevor leaned forward on the couch, purposely exposing his back.

Ardyce stopped dead in her tracks. Her jaw dropped, and then— *nothing*. The only sound was her sharp intake of air. Then she exploded. "I cannot believe you got a tattoo!" Ardyce choked out the words at a near yell. "What were you thinking, Trevor?"

Duaine shot out of his chair. "Let me see that!" He was all set to deride his son's stupidity, but caught himself in midshout. "Hey, that's actually pretty cool," he admitted. "I like it."

Ardyce was flabbergasted. Was she the only person in the room who thought the thing was disgusting?

"It could be worse," Duaine shrugged, looking at it again and touching it. "It's kind of manly."

She was speechless. It was pointless to argue, though. She sensed that Trevor was getting a certain thrill from shocking her. "Well, Trevor, just know that no matter how old I get, I will always be willing to pay for it to come off," she finally managed.

"Oh, it's not coming off, Mom. You might as well get used to it," Trevor said.

Chapter 7

The spring days were warming slightly, and the earthy, grassy smell of baseball filled the air. With the baseball season fast approaching, Trevor was eager to make his mark. He wanted everybody to know that not only was he the life of the party but that he was also an ace on the mound. He really looked forward to the girls in the stands cheering for him.

But there was a problem. Trevor's left elbow hurt. During practices he found himself favoring it a little, and it wasn't getting any better. Most of the time it really didn't hurt, and as he stepped onto the mound for his first start for the Lopers, he hoped he could ignore the pain.

Catcher Derek Appleton signaled for a curveball, and Trevor spun into his windup. As he gripped the ball and twisted, the dull ache in his elbow returned. He willed himself to control the ball, but it didn't work—it went straight in over the plate, and the batter sent it flying into the atmosphere for a home run. When he looked around at the girls in the stands, they were laughing at him, not cheering. He glanced toward his dad near the first baseline. Duaine's face looked as if it were set in stone, and his jaw twitched as he unconsciously gritted his teeth. "C'mon, Trevor!" he yelled. "Just relax. You'll be fine."

But Trevor didn't feel fine. A heavy sense of foreboding swept over him.

Derek ran out to the mound. "Hey, is everything all right? Do we need to change our approach?"

"Actually, my elbow is really bothering me," Trevor admitted. "Let's just stick to some simple pitches and see if I can get into my rhythm after a while."

"All right," Derek agreed. "We'll try that."

But the elbow didn't get any better, and neither did Trevor's pitching. After giving up three runs in the first inning, Coach Guy Murray pulled him. "What's the matter?" he asked.

"Oh, I guess I just practiced too hard. I was kind of excited to get started," Trevor said nonchalantly. "I'm a little sore; I should be OK with a little rest."

At the end of the game Trevor just waved to his dad and ran back to the locker room. He didn't want to deal with his dad's worrying about him. Certainly things would get better eventually—at least he hoped they would.

A week later Coach Murray approached Trevor in the dugout. "I'd like to start you again today. Do you feel up to it?"

"Sure! Let me at 'em!" Trevor said with enthusiasm. Even though his elbow still hurt when he moved certain ways, it really did feel better.

A soft breeze blew the scent of spring blossoms across the field, and with the sun on his back Trevor felt optimistic. As he ran out to the mound he was confident that this time he'd keep things together. He turned to look toward his dad, nodded a greeting, and then looked in for the sign. A changeup. Trevor delivered for a strike. Yes, things were looking pretty good. It might have been luck, but he got out of the first inning without giving up a run.

Back at the dugout Trevor's roommate cornered him. "Hey, T-Bull, something's still not right with you."

"What do you mean?" Trevor asked defensively.

"Well, you're sure sending me more balls into the outfield than I usually have to catch. I didn't think that was your style," Michael answered evenly.

"Yeah, well, thanks for catching 'em," Trevor retorted. "That's what you're supposed to do."

"What's going on here, guys?" Coach Murray interrupted.

"Trevor's still not showing us his best stuff," Michael said.

The coach looked at Trevor. "Michael has a point. You *are* letting them make contact pretty often."

Without thinking, Trevor rubbed his elbow. It felt kind of stiff, and it did hurt now that he thought about it.

"I'll tell you what," the coach said. "I'll let you go back out there, but the minute I get uncomfortable I'm pulling you."

"All right, Coach," Trevor mumbled.

Back on the mound, Trevor was determined not to give the batter anything to hit. Again and again he pitched balls, trying to snag the corner of the plate, but his arm was stiff, and he just couldn't make the ball go where he wanted it. He walked one, then two, batters. With two runners on base he threw a fastball down the center of the plate. The batter smacked a line drive into center field, and Max Sample dove and missed. One runner scored before the second runner was tagged, coming into third, for the first out.

Coach Murray jogged to the mound. "Trevor, it's time to come out. And I want you to have that elbow looked at."

Glancing over at his dad, Trevor said, "I think I'll go right now. I'm sure my dad will take me to have it checked out."

☆ ☆ ☆

Trevor's freshman season was over. He had a terrible 15.43 earned-run average (ERA) and couldn't do anything to fix it. The doctor said he had an inflamed ulnar collateral ligament, something like tennis elbow. Evidently it was very common in athletes who do a lot of gripping and twisting with their arms. He'd need surgery to fix it, and he wouldn't be able to pitch again for seven months.

"This is so frustrating!" Trevor fumed to his mom over the phone. "After the surgery I can do only nonstrenuous weights and exercises. I feel as if I'm never going to pitch again!"

"It'll be OK," Ardyce soothed. "I'll be praying for you. God will help you to be your best. Sometimes it's the difficult times that make us better people. You just have to have faith."

Trevor appreciated his mother's words, but he wasn't sure faith had much to do with baseball. He believed in success through hard work. Obviously God didn't always give you what you wanted, and he wasn't sure he wanted to give up control of his future to something as flimsy as faith.

That summer Trevor moved back to Lincoln, where he and Aaron worked for a plumbing company. They had a good time together working at a condominium construction site, and after work they partied.

The summer blew by quickly. When he returned to Kearney in the fall, Trevor was recruited to join the Pi Kappa Alpha fraternity. It sounded like a great way to party, but his baseball teammates heckled him for joining.

"You don't have to join a frat to have fun around here," fellow pitcher Josh Tolbert chided. "The baseball team knows how to party plenty hard. In fact, sometimes a coach will even have the team over for a kegger," he added with an amused chuckle.

Josh was right. So after one semester Trevor left the fraternity, and his reputation as a party animal only grew.

But the smallest change began taking place in Trevor's life that year. Ardyce had been praying faithfully for her son—and meddling a bit. She introduced him to Jill Danielson, a Seventh-day Adventist girl who attended Union College in Lincoln. The truth was Trevor thought she was kind of cute, and nice to be with. Boring perhaps, but nice. Like the majority of Seventh-day Adventists, Jill didn't drink, and she didn't party on Friday nights. She kept the Sabbath from sundown Friday night to sundown Saturday night. In some ways it made Trevor want to study the Bible a little more just so he could spend some time with her. And since she was in Lincoln, he didn't have to let her know about his double life. He could leave the drinking and parties at Kearney.

One afternoon after church Trevor called Jill. "Hey, do you want to come over to my parents' house so we can talk a little bit about the Bible? It seems like you know a lot about it, and I could probably learn something from you."

Jill covered the phone with her hand and turned to her roommate. "Carrie," she whispered, "I cannot believe this! Do you remember that guy I was telling you about who I thought was so good-looking? He's on the phone!"

"Well, what does he want?"

"He wants me to come over and study the Bible with him."

"So what's stopping you? I don't think I can think of a better way to spend the afternoon!" Carrie laughed. "Go! Get out of here."

"All right, Trevor," Jill agreed, turning back to the phone. "How do I get to your place?"

57

A few minutes later Trevor greeted her at the door with a kind of sideways hug. "Hey! How ya doin'?"

"I'm good," Jill smiled.

They stared at each other for a moment of awkward silence, then Trevor motioned her into the living room.

"What did you want to study?" Jill asked.

"I don't know," Trevor admitted. "I guess I'm just tired of living with guilt. Sometimes being popular makes me do some pretty stupid things. Does the Bible talk about anything like that?"

"Well, yes," Jill said. "But I hope you know that nobody expects you to be perfect. We all make mistakes. And Satan is the accuser. He's the one who makes us feel guilty. But Jesus took our place when He died on the cross, and now His perfect life replaces our life filled with mistakes, and Satan no longer can accuse us of anything."

Trevor nodded. Even if some of what Jill was saying sounded like a bunch of clichéd "churchspeak," he really enjoyed seeing the passion that came over her face when she spoke.

"Romans is a good place to look for what the Bible says on this subject," Jill continued, opening the *New Living Translation* she held on her lap. "I find this version very readable and easy to understand." She flipped through the pages and began to read Romans 5:6-9, NLT: "'When we were utterly helpless, Christ came at just the right time and died for us sinners. Now, no one is likely to die for a good person, though someone might be willing to die for a person who is especially good. But God showed his great love for us by sending Christ to die for us while we were still sinners. And since we have been made right in God's sight by the blood of Christ, he will certainly save us from God's judgment.'"

As she continued to read, Trevor's concentration drifted. He really liked the idea that he didn't have to worry about being a sinner. A feeling of peace came over him, and he began to tell himself that God knew his heart. Hopefully, if he kept going to church a little more often and seeing Jill, maybe it wouldn't matter that he still loved to party.

Jill stopped reading and looked up at him with an inquiring look.

"That was really good," Trevor said quickly. "Thanks for reading that to me." He gave her a sheepish grin. "I'd really like to see you more. Would you like to go to a movie, or go bowling or something, tonight?"

"Sure; that sounds really fun." Jill hoped she didn't sound too gushy. "Great. I'll pick you up at your dorm right after sundown."

☆ ☆ ☆

Trevor saw more of Jill throughout his sophomore year. He often spent Friday nights drinking and partying with his friends, then struggled to drag himself out of bed to go to church with Jill and his mother the next day.

For Christmas Trevor's aunt and uncle gave him Max Lucado's book *In the Grip of Grace*. It was the first Christian book Trevor read all the way through. Of course, it helped that they had placed $20 bills at the end of each chapter. They did the same with Ellen White's *Steps to Christ*. Even so, as he read Trevor came to understand better the impact of what Christ had suffered for him and other sinners at Calvary. He wanted to make better choices in his life. Although he was beginning to understand the sacrifice Jesus had made for him, he wasn't yet willing to make sacrifices of his own for Jesus. He was too self-centered to be friends with Jesus, and he still found more connection at parties than he did at church. Although the alcohol didn't fill his soul, it somehow made the emptiness feel numb. So actually making a change didn't feel possible, or even seem necessary. He reasoned that he was living the best life he could, and although his heart was beginning to be stirred, his priorities remained about the same.

By the end of the year he and Jill had broken things off, but a new, small flame had been kindled in Trevor's heart. He was baptized on May 31, 1997, the same day as his grandparents' sixtieth wedding anniversary.

Trevor still had another thing to learn about taking care of his mind and body. Healthy living wasn't just a benefit to his spiritual life; it mattered to his baseball career, too. Although his sophomore season easily topped his injured freshman season, it was no reflection of his true abilities as an athlete. The alcohol and intense living were taking their toll. He struggled on the mound, finishing with three wins and five losses credited to his record. His ERA average in 13 games was 6.67. The Lopers ended 1997 with 23 wins and 29 losses.

Chapter 8

"Hey, Michael!" Trevor called through the door to his roommate. "A couple guys from the team and I are off to get a keg of beer."

"All right, man!" Michael hollered back. It was great being Trevor's roommate. Never a dull moment.

Evening had descended on the campus, and the smell of damp leaves filled the cool air as Trevor inhaled deeply and set his mind to the night ahead. Patting his pocket, he made sure he had the fake ID he needed to get the keg. He wouldn't be 21 until January, but he was a junior now and a seasoned host.

People started showing up for the Friday night party a little before 9:00. Teammates and the girls they were seeing. Classmates and friends of classmates. Neighbors and other athletes. Sorority sisters and fraternity brothers and anyone else, it seemed, found their way to Trevor and Michael's place for the party. Soon the rooms were packed to overflowing with drunk and loosely inhibited college students.

"Wow! I cannot believe this!" Trevor shouted to Michael above the general din of voices. "I put up flyers only this afternoon—and I put up only *three* flyers. This is just insane! But in a good way," he added with a laugh.

"Well, T-Bull, you've established yourself in this town as a guy to party with!" Michael shouted back with a happy grin.

Trevor shook his head and laughed. He'd have to find some way to get a little more drunk, otherwise this stuffy, crowded atmosphere was going to get annoying after a while.

Inching his way across the room toward the keg, Trevor became aware of a strange sensation, as if he were falling. That didn't usually happen when he got drunk. It felt as if the floor were rumbling from a passing freight train or something, and people around him were beginning to topple into each other and into him. Punctuating the confused outbursts that were erupting all around him was a loud cracking sound mixed with wrenching and popping as electrical cords and their sockets were yanked from the wall.

He suddenly found himself in a heap of bodies, and it began to dawn on him that the floor had collapsed, cracking right down the middle. The whole party, it seemed, had slid to the middle of the room, which was now more like a jagged valley in the center of what had, moments before, been his home.

A shocked silence descended on the masses, followed by a ripple of squirming and nervous laughter. Wiggling out from under a sprawled girl, Trevor called, "You OK, Michael?"

"Yes," Michael responded, trying to swim over the bodies toward Trevor. "But dude, you've got to get rid of the keg. It's registered in our names."

They hurriedly threw the keg into a dumpster, and within minutes Kearney police officers and emergency personnel arrived on the scene. They treated several students, then dispersed the crowd.

And in the nearby dumpster they found the keg registered to Trevor and Michael.

The news article in the Kearney paper focused on the baseball team's connection and how the party truly could have been fatal. That night Trevor prayed the same prayer he prayed every night: a mindless collection of words thrust heavenward in the vain hope that somehow the act of uttering them made everything OK.

Back at the Kearney police station, Lieutenant Scott Harris was fuming. "You know who that kid was, don't you?" he sputtered in disgust. "That's Captain Duaine Bullock's son!"

"The narc captain from Lincoln?" Lieutenant Alan Glantz asked in surprise.

"That's the one. That kid is his son."

"And you couldn't slap him with a minor in possession charge?"

"Nope! He wasn't *actually* in possession when we found the keg." Harris sighed in frustration. "But we'll get him. We'll make sure we get it right. I promise you, we *are* going to bag little Bullock."

☆ ☆ ☆

Trevor stood in the side yard with a couple friends at a teammate's house. He held a can of beer in each hand as he scanned the area for girls. It was another Friday night, another party, another chance to get drunk. And it would be another morning of waking up in the arms of some girl who didn't look half as good in the morning light as she had looked the night before.

A couple guys approached Trevor. "Hey! Are you Trevor Bullock? I've heard about you, man!" one of them said with a broad smile. "Do you think you can round me up a chick or two?"

"Sure, that's me!" Trevor laughed. He hooked a thumb toward the house. "I think a lot of the girls are inside."

"Where'd you get the beers?" the other guy asked. "I'm ready to get sloshed. It's been a long week."

"The beer's inside, too. Follow me. Let's see what we find."

Trevor turned to lead the pair into the house. Behind his head, just a little too close, Trevor heard the first guy say, "OK, Bullock; put your hands behind your back!"

Trevor's teammates, who had minutes before been shooting the breeze with him, took off running. But holding his two open beer cans, Trevor was had.

"So, that's it, huh?" he muttered. "That's how it happens. I am such an idiot!"

The two plainclothes cops ushered Trevor to their car and cited him for being an MIP (a minor in possession of alcohol). Thoroughly warned that a repeat offense would not be tolerated, Trevor made his way home. He'd give his dad a call. Maybe the older Bullock would help him out.

When he reached his apartment, Trevor went straight to the phone and dialed the number. "Hey, Dad, listen. I kinda need your help. I got cited tonight for an MIP, and I was sort of hoping—"

The phone went dead. Duaine had hung up.

"Don't tell me that was a telemarketer at this hour," Ardyce quipped, looking over her glasses at her husband.

"No; that was our brilliant son!" Duaine said. "I told him before he ever went to Kearney that he needed to knock off his drinking. But did he? Nooooo!"

"So what happened?" Ardyce didn't know whether to be mad or worried.

"He got busted for being an MIP." Duaine crashed his fist into the arm of his favorite chair as he spat out the words.

"I'd like to hit him over the head right now!" Ardyce's anger and worry suddenly landed with a thud in the pit of her stomach. How could Trevor be so stupid? Didn't he understand that his choices in life impacted his ability to play baseball, his ability to reach his goals? There was no way to put into words all that she was feeling, but she was angry.

"I guess he still hasn't figured out that there are consequences for actions," Duaine sighed. "He's been pushing the limits for a long time. I'm a little surprised it took him this long to get arrested."

Ardyce eyed her husband suspiciously. "Are you telling me you *knew* Trevor was throwing away his future?"

"Well, I didn't *know* it exactly, but sometimes I'd hear things about him from the other cops, stuff I couldn't really substantiate. And you know cops like to talk, so . . ." His voice trailed off. "Listen, every kid hides things from his parents. I'm sure there's a lot of stuff we don't know about for certain."

Ardyce wasn't mollified. She leveled an accusing glare at Duaine.

"Don't worry, Ardyce; he'll be fine," Duaine said. "This might be what he needs to get his attention. A little jail time might do him some good."

☆ ☆ ☆

Duaine attended the court hearing with Trevor. He knew the judge, and he knew the prosecuting attorney, but he didn't say a word to either of them. Trevor pled guilty to the charges, and the Bullocks paid a fine of $175, plus $100 bail. Trevor was to spend the next weekend in jail.

On Friday night Trevor entered the booking area of the Kearney Police Department to begin serving his sentence. The officers laughed and jeered at him.

"Look what we got here!" Lieutenant Harris called out, standing up. "Bullock! Bullock! Bullock's boy! What a wonderful night this has turned out to be!"

Other Kearney officers throughout the building glanced at the TV monitor showing Trevor's face and snickered. Word spread to officers patrolling the streets, and they called in congratulatory jokes about jailing "little Bullock."

Officer Jack Braswell escorted Trevor into the fingerprint and photography area, then he was taken to the jail holding area before finally being put in a general cell. Two older, non-English-speaking Hispanic men were already there. A toilet sat in the middle of the cell.

The minutes ticked away slowly. Trevor read truck magazines, the only reading material to be had. He ate pancakes for breakfast and, later on, a Salisbury steak. But he wasn't about to use the toilet in the middle of the cell.

That night his mother didn't sleep much. She prayed, and thought about her son.

When Sunday evening finally rolled around, Trevor called Michael to come pick him up, but got no answer. So he walked to his apartment. Because he was a minor, the jail time didn't go on his permanent record, and Coach Murray remained ignorant of the antics of his cocky young pitcher.

Chapter 9

One thing did get Trevor's attention his junior year at Kearney: Ashleigh Meyer, an attractive blond. Trevor really thought he loved her. He thought he might marry her. But it was a lot like the way Trevor loved Jesus. Though he loved Jesus, that love was never of the variety that would lend itself toward a single-minded commitment, and though he loved Ashleigh, his love for her never deterred him from seeking the pleasure of other women's company.

There was, of course, the reality that Ashleigh was nothing at all like Jesus in the way she loved Trevor in return. She wasn't slow to enjoy the other players on the baseball team. And, if it was possible, she drank and partied more than Trevor did.

Troublesome Ashleigh (or "Fluff," as Trevor's mom called her) came from a rich family. Everything came easily to her, including a home that her parents had purchased for her. Trevor was quite smitten by her, but her love of alcohol was getting old.

"Have you looked at this place?" Trevor asked Ashleigh one morning after a particularly wild party. "Everywhere you look there are beer bottles and dirty dishes. We gotta find some friends who aren't slobs. This is ridiculous!" Clearly it was going to take him the whole morning to clean up, and Ashleigh was in no condition to help.

"Oh, shut up!" Ashleigh moaned. "You sound like my mom! It's not that big a deal. Do the best you can; then I'll do the rest when I get up."

"That's what you always promise, but you never do it," Trevor snapped. "Look at yourself! Your makeup is smeared. You've spilled beer in your hair—and in the bed. And I can still smell your nasty vomit from last night because you didn't flush the toilet. I'm so sick of this!"

65

Ashleigh grabbed a pillow and propped herself up in the disheveled bed. "What's happened to you, Trevor? You used to be so much more cool. You used to like getting plowed as much as I do. You never used to mind the messes I made. All you ever do now is nag."

"I complain because all I ever seem to do around here is clean up after you and your freeloading friends!" Trevor retorted. "I'm so beyond sick of this! I thought we had something, but really, all we had was a love of partying and playing house. All you seem to do is drink. Because of you I don't even like drinking anymore."

"I can't help it if you feel guilty every time you drink because of all those religious books you read," Ashleigh scoffed. "You don't see me looking at that hypocritical junk. College is about drinking, parties, and havin' a good time—not feeling guilty every time you turn around. My pretentious mother makes me feel guilty enough."

"Your drinking wouldn't be so bad if that was all that drove me crazy!" Trevor yelled. "Is there a guy you don't try to make out with? I saw you with your arms around *two* dudes last night when you were getting hammered. And no, you weren't steadying yourself. What's even worse is that both of those guys are my teammates. They're total players—and *you* were kissing *them!*"

"Oh, you should talk, Trevor." Ashleigh's voice had some fire now. "I always see you with girls. And most of them have worse reputations than I do. So don't tell me about my flirting—you don't just say hello either!" Ashleigh's head was pounding, but she had a point to make, and nothing was going to slow her torrent of words. "Trevor, you make out with some of these girls behind my back. You wanna know how I know? Most of the trashy girls shoot their mouths off about being with you. That's how low-class they are. And you keep falling for them! What do your Bible books say about that, huh?"

Trevor opened his mouth, but Ashleigh wasn't finished.

"I know I'm far from perfect, but at least I don't try to pretend to be somebody I'm not," she sneered. "Why do you even bother going to church? All church does to me is make me feel guilty, dirty, and worthless. Everywhere you go, self-righteous 'Christians' look down on you. They act as if they're so much better. *Gimme a break!*"

Trevor stared at her. This fluffy-haired, hungover blond was speaking the truth, and he knew it. "I go to church because I wish it *would* make me feel better," he said quietly. "It might make you feel better, though, if you took it more seriously and actually wanted to be a better person."

Truth to tell, he didn't really want to keep living this life. He hated what he saw of himself reflected in Ashleigh's accusations. And he was getting sick of sneaking around and trying not to get caught.

☆ ☆ ☆

If it seemed that Trevor was slowly moving toward making better choices in life, the same was true of his improvements on the baseball field. Subtle improvements, but improvements nonetheless. And though he wasn't impressed with the coaching he received in the Kearney program, what could his numbers have been without the drink and parties?

Because the Kearney coaching staff was made up primarily of assistant coaches who were fifth-year seniors, Trevor decided to take his cues from videotapes of some of the best University of Nebraska left-handed pitchers. Duaine taped the pitchers from the stands at home games in Lincoln, then sent them to Trevor, saying, "Go ahead and copycat what they're doing. This will help you see what we can change."

In this way Trevor did a lot of work on his own. He became motivated to improve by an intense rivalry with a teammate over who would be named the best player on the team. He developed more arm strength and put more velocity on the ball. He ended his junior year with a 6.48 ERA, with five wins and three losses credited to him. The team finished with 20 wins and 22 losses overall.

☆ ☆ ☆

Trevor buckled down his senior year at Kearney. During the first three years his social life had always come first, but he still had an ultimate goal of playing professional ball. The reality that this might be his final year of baseball unless something changed caused him to approach his career with a new determination.

Dating "Fluff" had sobered him up, and the results came through on the mound. By the end of his senior season he led his conference with a 1.64 ERA. He had dealt 78 strikes and issued only 18 walks in 66 innings pitched. He had nine starts and pitched eight complete games.

Coach Murray noticed that Trevor didn't walk batters so often. Where he had previously been hit-and-miss with his pitches, now there was a complete turnaround. He was showing a whole different kind of purpose.

With the exception of one thing. Trevor wasn't quite ready to give up his bad-boy image, so he got a tongue ring. Duaine had been OK with the tattoo, but he hated the ring. And so did the coach, so Trevor wasn't allowed to wear it when he played ball.

This new determination seemed to fuel one other negative—his temper. Even though his stats were impressive and he had attained his goal of having an ERA under 2.00, it really grated on his nerves how many errors were being committed behind him.

"I can't do this entirely on my own!" Trevor yelled after watching a fly ball to left fielder Zac Henderson get misplayed and go to the left-field fence. Trevor stood helpless in frustration as two runs scored. The Lopers were only one out away from sewing up the inning.

Coach Murray trotted out to the mound to calm down his ace. down. "You can't go yelling at your teammates when you're on the mound. You just can't!" Murray bellowed, swinging his arms out in wide animated arcs. "Errors happen, and you gotta not let 'em bother you. I know you had a shutout going, but that's gone now. You gotta focus on the guy coming up and forget everything else. You got that, T-Bull?"

"All right; I'll make it happen," Trevor said, wiping the sweat off his forehead. "It's just that these guys don't look like they're trying hard enough."

"Trevor, I don't want to hear it," Coach Murray huffed as he walked away. "Focus on the batter!"

"This is such garbage!" Trevor muttered as he stepped back onto the mound. Glancing at his infielders, he thought about how much better he was than this team. He had worked his tail off all season for a losing team. What a dump! He was glad to be getting out soon.

Just then he heard his dad whistle from the first baseline. "OK," he whispered to himself. "Just get out of this inning."

With two fastballs and a curve, Trevor struck the final batter out and headed for the dugout. "You call that defense?" he yelled to no one in particular. "This is ridiculous! Now would be a great time for you guys to redeem yourselves by getting some runs."

"Bullock, just shut up!" catcher Luis Mabry demanded. "Nobody wants to hear it. Just shut up!"

Trevor's hysterics didn't change anything. The first three batters on his team went down in order to end the inning. He pitched well the rest of the game and didn't allow a hit, walking only two batters. Even so, Kearney wasn't able to generate any more offense and lost the game 2-1.

After it was over, Trevor trotted to the fence to greet his parents. "Another great game by me, and another loss credited to my record," he grumbled. "This team just doesn't get any better."

Unfortunately, Trevor was right. In spite of his stellar season Kearney finished 1999 with the worst record they had ever sported in the four years Trevor had played with them: 18 wins and 27 losses. Trevor himself had five wins and five losses on his record, even though he gave up very few runs. In an effort to rise above his team he attended open tryouts for major league baseball at various times during the season. But nothing came of it.

☆ ☆ ☆

"What is wrong with you?" Coach Murray yelled.

Trevor had just shown up at the Kearney team banquet with his tongue ring in.

Trevor brushed him off. "Coach, no one will know."

Coach Murray was furious. "If I know, everyone knows!" The nerve! They were here to celebrate the good things about the season and the team in the home of an alumnus of the baseball team, and

Trevor had inserted one final, self-important jab of disrespect and cynicism. He waved Trevor off in disgust and walked away.

Trevor's senior year at Kearney was over. He hadn't earned a degree yet, and with his college baseball career coming to an end, uncertainty swirled all around him. Fortunately, he had shown enough promise during his senior season to be noticed by some scouts for a summer league that recruited top college baseball players in Nebraska. Hoping to be noticed, he spent the summer playing in the league for the Beatrice Bruins under coach Bob Steinkamp.

In addition to being the coach of the Bruins, Steinkamp was a scout for the Seattle Mariners. Other scouts from major league baseball were watching too. If Trevor was hoping to be noticed, he had come to the right place. But unlike at Kearney, he was going to have to work hard to stick out. There were many top athletes strutting their stuff with the same hopes he had.

☆ ☆ ☆

"Did you say the *pitcher* is your son?" Larry Armstrong asked. He was watching a Bruins game from Duaine's favorite first baseline spot. Armstrong's son, Kade, was Trevor's teammate.

"Yeah, that's him," Duaine confirmed. "He's doing well out there, but I'm a little worried that it won't be enough."

"He's doing *great*!" Larry encouraged. "But you might be right—there are many talented kids out here. It's hard to stick out and be noticed."

"It's just so disappointing!" Duaine said, making a fist. "He played at Kearney for a dreadful team with no real guidance. How was he supposed to get better and be noticed out there? And then his freshman season was a total waste. He injured his elbow and pitched only three innings the whole season."

"So how many full seasons did he pitch for Kearney?"

"Full seasons? Uh, let's see . . . three."

"He can apply for a medical redshirt!" Larry exclaimed enthusiastically. "He really should! If his freshman season was such a waste, then you should have no problem getting an extra year of eligibility. Maybe he could play for the Cornhuskers! Your son has a special gift; I can see it. You really need to get that extra year."

"Trevor, you gotta do this!" Duaine urged after the game. "You could transfer from Kearney to Lincoln and play a year for the Huskers. You might actually have some good coaches who will help you."

Trevor shook his head. "I don't know, Dad. I suppose Coach Steinkamp might put in a good word for me with the Huskers, but I don't want another year of college eligibility; I want a major league team to notice me."

"Well, you don't *have* to play at the college level for another year, but if you get the eligibility you have the option to play college ball," Duaine reasoned. "If no pro scouts notice you *here*, you'll still have some place to play ball, a place better than Kearney and where pro scouts are watching more closely."

With a resigned shrug Trevor agreed.

During the next several days he helped his dad compile medical records and other data needed to apply to the NCAA for an extra year of eligibility. In the end, his fifth year of eligibility was granted. And with a good word from Coach Steinkamp, he was allowed to play baseball for the Cornhuskers at the University of Nebraska as a walk-on player. No scholarships were available by the time his eligibility was granted, but that didn't matter. He was ready to show off how good he was. In fact, he was already doing so with the Beatrice Bruins.

Late in the summer season the Bruins went to the National Baseball Congress World Series in Wichita, Kansas. Stepping onto the mound against the Edmond, Oklahoma, Mudcats, Trevor looked around, hoping to see the herd of scouts. Duaine inhabited his usual post on the first baseline, and Ardyce sat in the stands. Already the Bruins had accumulated three runs in the top of the first inning.

Trevor's first pitch was a four-seam fastball, straight in over the plate, to Tommy Simmons. Hoping to start strong, Simmons swung, sending a screamer straight back to Trevor. Before Trevor even had a conscious thought of it, his glove shot out and snagged the ball for the first out of the inning. A slight smirk flickered at the corner of his mouth, then disappeared again behind his well-perfected game face. It was going to take more than an aggressive first batter to throw him out of his rhythm today.

As he looked at the next batter, Trevor heard Ardyce yell, "Give him the dark one!" She was always yelling that. She wanted Trevor to deliver a pitch that the batter couldn't see. Hearing her voice waft out from the stands made him laugh. It didn't matter where he was—he could count on his dad to whistle at him and his mom to ask for the dark one.

Turning into his windup, Trevor uncoiled a heater that flew over the plate for a strike, the dark one Ardyce had been asking for. If Simmons had been eager to swing, the second batter, Jacob Lumpkin, was not. Trevor delivered two more fastballs over the plate, and each time they were called as strikes. Lumpkin had struck out looking.

Again and again Trevor sent the ball flying for a strike. Five of the first six outs were strikeouts by Trevor. He was on fire. Sometimes a batter would get a little bat on the ball, but each fly ball was easily caught, and the Mudcats remained scoreless.

In the middle of the third inning the coach for the Mudcats inserted Donald Sewell, a lefty batter, to pinch-hit against Trevor. Maybe putting the batter on the other side of the plate would throw off Trevor's concentration. It was worth a try.

Looking in for the sign, Trevor pretended nothing was different. His determination to dominate wasn't going to be altered by a lefty batter. "You're just desperate," he muttered under his breath. Closing his eyes, he decided just to put the ball where he knew it needed to go. Duaine had practiced this with him hundreds of times, pitching by feel, with his eyes closed. In fact, if he closed his eyes he could almost feel as if he were back home in Lincoln with his dad.

Inhaling deeply, Trevor sent a two-seam fastball in over the outside corner of the plate. Sewell swung, sending an unexpected grounder dribbling into right field. Tony Dutter sprinted in, scooped up the ball, and hurled it to first base, just in time to get Sewell out. Trevor nodded his approval to Tony. How nice it was to finally be playing on a team that the fielders helped you out from time to time.

While Trevor was striking out the Mudcats, his teammates were pounding out the runs. By the end of the fifth inning the Bruins were leading by a score of 10 to 0. Stepping onto home plate, the umpire called the game, invoking the 10-run "mercy" rule. The game was over.

"You hungry?" Duaine asked as Trevor sprinted over to his parents on the sidelines.

"Yes!" Trevor said. "Maybe I'll get a Sunkist orange soda like the ones I always used to drink after T-ball when I was little. I'm thirsty!" Trevor was feeling expansive after such a powerful routing. "Do you remember that Sunkist from the cooler at T-ball games, Mom? Doesn't that sound good right now?"

"Yes, I remember," Ardyce laughed. "And if it sounds good to you, then you can have it."

The tough-guy pitcher was definitely morphing back into the starry-eyed little boy. *Men never grow up,* Ardyce thought, smiling.

As the trio slid into their maroon Honda Accord, Trevor asked, "What did you think, Dad?"

"I thought you were good! What did you think I'd think of a no-hitter?"

"That was a no-hitter?" Trevor was running over everything in his head. Usually he did this sort of rehashing around the seventh or eighth innings, but since they had played only five innings he hadn't even noticed.

As if in response to Trevor's surprise, one of the Bruins coaches ran up to the Honda and tapped on the window. "You pitched a no-hitter!" he yelled. "Wow!"

Thanks to Dutter's fantastic help getting that one batter out at first, he had another no-hitter to credit to his record. It was the first no-hitter at the NBC World Series in six years.

Trevor was the starting pitcher for one other game during the tournament. At the end he had an ERA of 1.42 in 12⅔ innings. By comparison, future Chicago Cubs standout pitcher Mark Prior, who was also at the tournament, had an ERA of 1.64 in 11 innings.

Chapter 10

Trevor had a lot to learn. At Kearney he was a guaranteed starter. With the Cornhuskers he'd have to prove himself. At Kearney the 1999 season record was 18 wins and 27 losses. The Huskers had 42 wins and 18 losses. In short, they were a winning team, and they didn't need Trevor in order to be a winning team.

However, Trevor hadn't learned that yet. He really believed he would be an automatic hero. He had read Mitch Sherman's piece in the Omaha *World-Herald* that quoted Nebraska head coach Dave Van Horn: "We're real pleased to get Bullock. He had a nice summer and actually ended up being the best pitcher on the [Bruins] team." Trevor knew Coach Steinkamp had told the Nebraska coaches how good he was at striking people out, and that he had a nice curveball. These guys would *have* to be impressed!

But they weren't.

Trevor, on the other hand, *was* impressed. Stepping into his apartment one brisk fall evening, he flopped on the couch and looked brightly at Aaron. He and Aaron were rooming together again. They had hoped to pitch together also, but Aaron had run out of college eligibility.

Raising an eyebrow, Aaron asked, "What's gotten into you?"

"This baseball program is great!" Trevor looked almost conspiratorial, as if what he was about to say were some sort of marvelous secret. "At Kearney I had to buy my own shoes. Here, I opened my locker for the first time, and there were *three* pairs of shoes, just waiting for me!"

"Welcome to Division I," Aaron said dryly.

"But there's more!" Trevor's glee was not to be brushed aside. "The difference between this baseball program and Kearney's is like the difference between preschool and college. I've got a new uniform, new workout clothes, new glove, and new hat. It's like Christmas every week!" Trevor grinned broadly. Then slowly his expression faded. "I guess all this great stuff comes at a price, though."

"What's that supposed to mean?"

"They're running me to death," Trevor complained. "The *pitching* coach is making me do all these sprints and stuff. Doesn't he *know* I mostly use my *arm?*"

"Maybe he doesn't want you getting a charlie horse if you ever have to dive for the ball," Aaron replied glibly.

"Have I *ever* gotten a charlie horse diving for the ball?"

The truth of the matter was that Rob Childress, the pitching coach, didn't need a reason for running his players hard in the fall. He wanted to see what they were made of. And at the moment, whiny Trevor was not showing that he was made of the stuff Childress wanted.

But he was competitive. He wasn't about to be outdone by a pitching coach who ran fall practice like boot camp. With a glint of determination in his eye he looked straight at Aaron and said, "I'll show them. If they want me to run, I'll run!"

"You might have to stop drinking so much," Aaron suggested.

Trevor didn't even blink. "OK, then I will! When spring comes, I'm going to start the very first game."

Trevor did work hard. If he showed any signs of frustration with the training, Coach Childress would yell, "If you're not going to work hard and sell out to the team, then you should just quit!" So Trevor worked hard. Even so, the Cornhuskers coaching staff wasn't about to put their cocky new pitcher in as a starter. Trevor was a reliever. And he came out of the bullpen for a total of only 3⅓ innings during the first 10 games of the season.

Trotting over to talk with his dad following yet another game without any work, Trevor was visibly irritated. Everybody could see it. The coaches. The players. The fans. Everybody could see that Trevor was unhappy.

"Dad, what do they want from me? I'm one of the best pitchers on the team, and they won't use me *at all!*" Trevor fussed. "I've had three appearances, and I haven't given up an earned run in any of them!"

Duaine just shook his head. "I hear ya." He was frustrated too. He had come to all 10 games. "But don't let yourself get mad, OK? They won't put you in as a starter any faster if you get mad. Just make every appearance your best."

Trevor ran a hand through his hair and muttered, "OK. I'll see you at tomorrow's game." He turned and headed back to the athletic building.

Finally, in mid-March, Trevor got his first start with Nebraska. He pitched eight innings, allowed six hits, and gave up three runs. It was a strong start, but he found himself back in the bullpen again. Once again he was pitching for one inning here or a third of an inning there. Sometimes Childress brought him in to face only one batter.

Following a string of seven games in which he didn't pitch at all, Trevor's frustration reached a boiling point. Seeing him kicking around the training room in an obvious fit of self-pity, Coach Van Horn called Trevor and Coach Childress in for a closed-door meeting.

"Bullock, is there something you need to say?" Van Horn barked.

"Why didn't you put me in against Baylor?" Trevor fumed. "They swept us! I know I could have held them better than the guys you used as starters." He flung himself into the chair opposite Van Horn.

Childress eased into the chair next to him and waited for the inevitable explosion that he expected from Van Horn, and Van Horn did not disappoint.

"Are you trying to tell me you are better than Shane Komine?" The red was rising in Van Horn's neck. "Shane is our best starter, so I don't *ever* want to hear you say you're better than the guys we choose as starters. I don't owe you *anything!* You got that?"

Trevor cocked his head and held Van Horn in a steady gaze.

"Listen, Bullock, I only gave you a chance because Coach Childress here saw something in you last summer. But last summer was a long time ago. And as far as I'm concerned, you could go all season without an earned run and I wouldn't want you on my staff!"

"Let me make this clear for you, Trevor," Coach Childress added in a firm, even tone. "You need to keep your mouth shut. Work your tail off and do as you're told. If you don't like it here, you can just leave. Is that what you want?"

Trevor shook his head.

"All right; then keep your mouth shut and let your pitching do the talking. Now get out of here!"

Trevor lurched out of his chair.

"And one more thing, Bullock. If you throw well, you're going to get the ball. It's that simple."

"Yes, sir," Trevor mumbled as he shut the door.

Van Horn and Childress looked at each other and nodded. Hopefully this little talk would get Trevor in line. They both knew he had a lot of potential. They liked his heart and intensity, but he needed to harness it. They didn't want a prima donna southpaw strutting around in the dugout. The ego and selfishness needed to go.

"He'll fall in line," Childress said. "We're his best shot at playing in the bigs. If he screws this up, he'll never get there. And I think he knows that."

The "heart-to-heart" meeting paid off for Trevor—and for the team. His cocky attitude was replaced by an unwavering confidence in his ability to get the job done. In his second start he gave up five hits and three runs in seven innings to get the win over Creighton. His record with Nebraska was now three wins and no losses. Coach Van Horn was pleased.

Trevor earned another start that also went well. The next start did not. He got knocked around hard by Texas A&M and was yanked after 1⅔ innings and sent back to the bullpen.

This time Trevor vowed to give his best with every chance he was given. It wasn't long before he was just the man his team needed.

In a game against Wisconsin-Milwaukee the Huskers found themselves down 9-0 in the fourth inning with two runners on base. Trevor was called in.

"Yes!" Duaine whispered to himself from the first base line.

Trevor loosened up a little with catcher Justin Cowan, then signaled the umpire that he was ready. His first pitch was a fastball over the outside corner of the plate. The ump ruled it a ball.

From her perch in the stands Ardyce yelled, "Oh, c'mon, Blue!" She never agreed when an umpire thought her son threw balls. Even if a pitch wasn't a strike, it *should* have been a strike. So she'd yell. Unfortunately for her vocal cords, the next pitch was a ball too, as was the next, and the next. Trevor had walked the first batter he faced, and the bases were loaded.

In the shadows of the dugout Coach Van Horn stood up and took off his Oakley sunglasses. He willed Trevor to get them out of this pinch. He knew the young pitcher could do it. The question was, would he?

Some pitchers might have crumbled with the pressure of having the bases loaded, but Trevor's resolve to dominate only became stronger. He went on to pitch 5⅓ innings of perfect relief, not giving up a single run. Along the way he retired 16 batters in a row, striking out six.

It was masterful. Trevor had arrived.

Coach Childress was beaming. Turning to Van Horn, he said, "Did you see that? We've got our T-Bull!"

Even though the Huskers lost the game, everyone knew that Trevor had had an impressive outing.

"That was awesome!" Duaine was almost gushing.

Trevor smiled. It felt good to make his dad proud.

Wisconsin-Milwaukee player Chad Sadowski was waiting for Trevor when he turned around. "That was really great pitching," Sadowski acknowledged. "Your pitches are deceptive, and you're aggressive. Good job!"

The coaches decided to give Trevor more playing time. Some outings were better than others, but Trevor never lost his drive. Heading into the end of the season the Huskers picked up momentum, winning 24 of their final 27 games to advance to the Big 12 Conference Tournament in Oklahoma City.

☆ ☆ ☆

"Our boy is the starter in a *big* college game!" Ardyce cried gleefully.

It was the second game of the NCAA Regional Tournament. The Cornhuskers had won the Big 12 Conference and were now competing for the regional title. Coach Van Horn had decided to give Trevor a nod of approval, and put him in as the starter for game two against the Minnesota Gophers.

Scanning the stands, Duaine tried to count how many scouts were watching this game. He wanted so badly for Trevor to be noticed and picked up by a major league franchise. He was pleased that Trevor was starting for such an important game, but truthfully, it made him nervous, nervous that he'd have a bad day and that the scouts would never give him a chance. His son had worked hard and deserved the best— his son *was* the best.

As he ran out to the mound Trevor heard fellow pitcher R. D. Spiehs yell, "OK, T-Bull, send those little gophers scampering back into their hole!"

As he warmed up with Justin, he paused occasionally to look around Siebert Field. Approximately 1,000 Husker fans had made the trek to Minnesota to fill the stands with scarlet and cream. Trevor appreciated the support, but he wasn't looking in the stands to find the scarlet and cream. He still needed to find the pretty girls—it didn't matter what color they were wearing.

"Hey, T-Bull, you ready for this?" Justin had arrived on the mound.

"Oh, yeah," Trevor nodded. "I like the pressure of the big game. I'd rather be on the mound for a game like this than have to watch some other pitcher mess it up."

"All right," Justin said, waving off Trevor's arrogance. "You better give me the strikes I want or else I'm going to come out here and chew your tail!"

Justin returned to his crouch behind the plate and signaled for a slider. Trevor spun out of his windup and sent the ball zinging in over the inside of the plate. It was a ball.

Trevor shook his shoulders a little. He felt kind of stiff. Maybe jittery. He hadn't really placed the ball where he really wanted it. He pitched again, but he just wasn't on. The first two hitters grounded out. Then Trevor walked the Gophers' top hitter, Jack Hannahan, on five pitches.

Coach Childress motioned to the umpire and strode briskly to the mound to calm his star left-hander down. This game was too important to let it get away in the first inning.

The conversation was short. "You're better than this, Bully," Coach Childress said. "Just relax and have some fun."

"OK. Thanks, Coach." Looking around the stadium, he saw for the first time how many Husker fans there were. He also saw the scouts. Off to his left he heard Duaine whistle and suddenly felt warm and eager to get the job done. He settled down to strike out Josh Halthaus, Minnesota's cleanup hitter. He had made it out of the first inning without a blemish.

"No soup for you!" R.D. cracked from his seat in the bullpen.

Trevor returned to the dugout and took a deep breath and thought about how far he'd come. This game really was exciting. At least he was here with a good catcher and good fielders behind him. Coach Childress was right—he needed to have fun.

He trotted out to the mound in the second inning with a new-found sense of adventure. He walked leadoff hitter, Luke Appert, on five pitches. Then he struck out the next two batters. And even though Appert stole second, he was denied the opportunity to score when Jeremy Negen grounded out.

Trevor had seized control of the game.

Jason Kennedy came to the plate in the bottom of the eighth inning for the scoreless Gophers. He wanted a piece of Trevor. Shifting slightly in the batter's box, he drilled a hole into Trevor's chest with his unwavering gaze.

Trevor delivered the pitch: a fast curveball over the outside of the plate. Kennedy pivoted forward just slightly and brought the bat around to make stunning contact with the ball—a solo home run.

As Kennedy passed the Cornhusker bullpen, R.D. jeered, "Merely a flesh wound!"

Trevor pitched a complete game for the Huskers, leading them to a 4-1 win over the Gophers.

Duaine was pleased. Trevor had done it! He'd started slow, but he showed all the scouts that he could take charge of the game. Around him he heard some of the Gopher fans admit, "That Trevor Bullock pitched an outstanding game." As he made his way toward Trevor he overheard Minnesota's Kennedy granting an interview with the media. "He's one of the top pitchers we've faced." Duaine was thrilled indeed.

The next day, with the pitching of Jamie Rodrigue, the Huskers pounded Wichita State 8-1, grabbing the first regional title the school had ever won. They were going to Palo Alto, California, to face Stanford University in a best-of-three-game series for the Super Regional title!

"You're our starter for this first game against Stanford," Coach Van Horn told Trevor. "Shane's still resting that broken jaw he got in the Minneapolis regional."

Trevor grinned. He'd had only a four-day rest, but he was thrilled with every opportunity to display his confidence.

Over in the Stanford training room, machismo was being thrown around as well. "Look at this!" snorted Brandon Chambers. "Look at this quote in the Lincoln *Journal Star* by that full-of-himself Nebraska pitcher Trevor Bullock."

"What'd he say?" came a chorus of voices

"Let me read it to you!" Chambers smirked. Holding the paper grandly before his face, Chambers read Trevor's words: "'I'm pretty confident in what I can do. The closer the ball game, the better I pitch. If it's close, you're pretty much going to have to work to earn what you need. I'm not going to give up too much, not make too many mistakes.'"

"Oh-ho-ho-ho!" Wade McLeod laughed mockingly. "Let's just watch some more videos of this Bullock guy pitching. I'm sure we can help him make a few more mistakes. I think I've pretty much memorized his curveball. How about you guys?"

There was a general eruption of grunts and chuckles of agreement.

"Wait! There's more!" Chambers chortled. "You're going to love this! Bullock says, 'Deep down inside, I think that if I go out there and do my job I'm going to come out with a win.'" Chambers snickered. "Well, we shall just see about that!"

Trevor had no idea how prepared the Stanford players were, or maybe he simply underestimated their ability. But as he stepped onto the mound in Klein Field at Sunken Diamond in Stanford, he was about to find out what it was like to face a very talented team.

Craig Thompson stepped into the batter's box, as confident as Trevor was, and took his time. He watched the first three pitches—a strike and two balls. He was ready on the fourth pitch. Swinging the bat around, Thompson pelted the ball into center field for a single.

Trevor shook his head. This wasn't how he'd imagined it. The first batter he faced was now on first base. He was determined to get the next one, and did, when Eric Bruntlett hit a fly ball to center field for an out.

Nodding in satisfaction, Trevor relaxed. Things would fall into line. He was sure of it.

But they didn't.

The third batter, Edmund Muth, got the bat on the ball and sent it straight back to Trevor. It was a split-second bobble, but Trevor was thrown off and committed an error that allowed Muth to get to first base, and Thompson advanced to third.

Justin called a time-out and trotted out to the mound. "All right, Bullock, these guys are all over you. You're not placing the ball. Get it together, man!" As he turned to go back to the plate, he added, "Coach just signaled an intentional walk, so let's do it!"

"OK. We'll set up the double play."

Justin nodded and scampered back to home. Stepping to the side, he dutifully caught Trevor's next four pitches. Cleanup hitter John Gall ran to first. Now the bases were loaded.

Trevor closed his eyes and murmured, "Please, God, get us the double play."

However, when Joe Borchard hit a sacrifice fly to right field, Adam Shabala caught the ball but couldn't get it to any of the bases in time to turn the double play. Thompson scored.

Chris O'Riordan shot Trevor an amused smirk as he came to the plate. "Bet you didn't expect us to score in the first inning, did you, Mr. Hot Stuff?" he muttered to himself. He was just settling in to watch what Trevor had to offer, when the pitch came way inside. He danced away to avoid the hit, but got plunked anyway. Tossing his bat to the side, he almost laughed out loud. Trevor had just given him a free ride to first, and the bases were loaded again. It was kind of fun yanking Trevor around!

Duaine groaned. This wasn't going well. He saw Justin storm out to the mound, flapping his arms wildly, and he knew Trevor was getting an earful. "C'mon, Trev," he breathed. "Get ahold of yourself."

The seventh batter hit a fly ball to right field for the final out.

Trevor had gotten through the inning, but it had been messy. In the dugout he asked for more time. "Coach Van Horn, I think I can do this. I think I can get settled down and make these guys pay."

"All right, T-Bull; I'm not pulling you yet, but I will as soon as I'm not comfortable."

Trevor nodded. With renewed determination he retired the first three batters in the second inning. Hopefully he had things under control now.

However, on the very first pitch of the third inning Bruntlett ripped the ball into left field and got on base. Then Muth fouled out. The Stanford players were simply getting their bats on the ball way too often for Van Horn's liking. He pulled Trevor and brought in R.D.

"I'm the king of the world!" R.D. crowed, raising his arms over his head. And he was. He pitched the rest of the game and got the win. But it wasn't enough.

The 2000 Husker baseball team went on to lose the next two games, placing second in the Super Region, and never got to go to the College World Series in their own backyard at Rosenblatt Stadium in Omaha. The Nebraska players took the final loss hard.

Coach Van Horn was waiting. "You men have been a team that has always hung in the game. You have nothing to be ashamed of," he thundered into the unhappy silence. "You've butted heads with some pretty big schools, and you've been winners. We beat Texas two out of three in Austin, and we placed second here. This program has made a lot of big strides, and I'm proud of the seniors who led us here. We hung in there for all three games. I'm proud to be your coach!"

Coach Childress nodded his agreement. "You guys are the best team I've ever coached."

The Cornhuskers had finished the 2000 season with 51 wins and 17 losses, and at 3.14 held the best team ERA in the nation. Trevor's 2.13 ERA was the best on the team.

☆ ☆ ☆

Trevor leaned back and stared out the window of the plane. It was really over . . . He was heading back to Lincoln after a thrilling season

83

and a lot of good times. His college baseball career was over, and he didn't have a clue what he was going to do with himself now. He still hadn't earned a college degree.

As the plane taxied into Lincoln Municipal Airport, Trevor smoothed out his rumpled Nebraska T-shirt. He'd wear his Cornhusker attire proudly, but it sure would be nice to play some more ball. For years baseball was all he'd thought about and dreamed of doing. He didn't want to be finished.

He grabbed his bag from the carry-on bin and thought how disappointed his dad must be right now. Since he had lived to watch Trevor play ball, Trevor wasn't even sure what he'd find to talk about with his dad now that he didn't have an active baseball career.

Sliding into his silver Jeep Cherokee, he slowly turned toward home. He hoped his mom would be waiting for him. He needed a kind word and a bit of encouragement to set his world in balance again. He needed—

The ringing of his cell phone jolted him from his thoughts.

"Trevor, this is Jerry Lafferty." The voice at the other end was cheerful. "I'm a scout for the Philadelphia Phillies, and I'd like to speak with you. Where are you right now?"

His pulse quickened. "I'm driving home." Could this be *the* call, the long-awaited call from a major league franchise?

"OK; well, you might want to pull over for this," Lafferty said. "The Phillies drafted you in the twenty-sixth round. Do you wanna sign?"

"Absolutely!" Trevor hollered.

"Great! Let me give you some of the details. We'll sign you to a typical seven-year minor league contract. You'll get $1,000 signing bonus and around $1,200 a month. We'll send you to play the 70-game short season in Batavia, New York, for the Class A Muckdogs."

Trevor expelled the huge breath of air he'd been holding and gasped, "Thank you!" He was in! *Yes! Yes! Yes!* He'd known that if he could just get in he'd be able to climb. All his hopes were finally being realized. He couldn't wait to tell his dad!

Trevor was 23 years old. He'd been a fifth-year college senior, and he was all out of college eligibility. The major league scouts knew they wouldn't have to throw a lot of money at him to get him to sign, so they hadn't. Trevor didn't care.

☆ ☆ ☆

Trevor boarded the plane and quickly located his seat. First class! *Yes!* He grinned at his seatmate, Matt Riethmaier, who'd been drafted in the fifth round and had previously played for the University of Arkansas. "Doesn't this feel great!"

"Yeah!" Matt agreed. "It almost feels like it's not really happening."

Once in Batavia, New York, which is halfway between Rochester and Buffalo, Trevor moved into a room in a big green Victorian house. The landlady had set up a couple beds for him and his roommate, Chad Sadowski. Chad was his former opponent from the Wisconsin-Milwaukee team.

If he had had a spare moment, Trevor could have gone to Niagara Falls—it wasn't far away. But he wasn't in Batavia for sightseeing. He quickly realized that everybody on the team, which included future all-star second baseman Chase Utley, was as good as he was. Maybe even better. And it was tough. On any given day a player could be there playing the game, and the next day he'd be cleaning out his locker.

Trevor determined he'd do everything he could to keep his job. He cut back even more on drinking and focused on his health and staying in shape. But there was still the matter of all the women who faithfully came to the games to pick up a good time. Certainly the pleasure of their company wasn't going to hurt anything. . . . And one thing was never in doubt: Trevor's stunning good looks drew women like a thirsty horse to a cool mountain stream.

His dreams were coming true, but still there was a nagging sense of emptiness that kept plaguing him. Most of the time it was subtle, and he could ignore it. Sometimes at night, though, he'd find himself praying the same old prayer he always prayed, and he wondered if God was really hearing him at all. The attention from all the willing women was really nice, but the pleasure was short-lived. And it seemed that more and more often he felt more and more alone.

One evening Trevor took a chance and expressed some of his malaise to his roommate.

"You know, this is kind of hard. We play all these games, and every day you have to worry about whether or not it's going to be your last day. It makes me feel tired."

"Yeah, it's kind of rough," Chad agreed.

"I'm kind of glad my mom prays for me," Trevor went on. "My dad is the captain of the narcotics unit in Lincoln, so pretty much my mom is the nice one, if you know what I mean."

"You're mom *prays* for you?" Chad's voice carried a hint of sarcasm. "And that makes you feel *better?*"

"Well, yeah. She prays for my dad, too. I think it's kind of nice. I mean, with all the stupid stuff I do it's probably a good thing she prays. Besides, I'm a Christian too, and I pray sometimes . . ." His voice trailed off.

"All right, Bullock, I got it. You don't have to talk about Jesus anymore with me. It's all a load of trash, and I don't want to hear it—especially from my roommate. Give me a break!"

"OK, relax, Chad!" Trevor said quickly. "I'm not preaching at you. I hate it when people force me to endure a lot of fake, mindless Jesus talk. I was just telling you about my mom." Changing the subject, he said, "C'mon, let's go get some of those amazing chicken fingers at Tully's."

"Dude, we went there last night!" Chad complained. Then he caught himself. Tully's did have the best chicken fingers he had ever tasted. And he actually did think they sounded good—again. He sat up and pulled on his shoes. "Oh, all right, I'll come," he said agreeably.

Trevor's commitment and drive brought him success during the 2½-month season with the Muckdogs. He split his time between starting and being a reliever. By the end of the season he had pitched 62 innings with 54 strikeouts. His ERA was 2.61, with six wins and three losses credited to him. With 39 wins and 37 losses, the Muckdogs ended the season in second place in the Pinckey Division of the New York-Penn League.

Chapter 11

The boisterous—and soused—crowd of Husker fans was just beginning to croon "There Is No Place Like Nebraska" when Trevor and Aaron stepped into Sidetrack. The sparsely decorated club, packed with passionate Nebraska fans, was getting revved up for the football game the following afternoon. Joyce Durand had taken her place at the keyboard to lead the tuneful revelers in her usual quirky way.

Looking for a good time during the off-season, Trevor and Aaron had come into downtown Lincoln to see what the scene had to offer. They ended up at Sidetrack. As he scanned the crowd, Trevor's eyes lingered on a slim, attractive blond in a leopard-print top and black pants. Her short, almost boyish hair made her look a little like Meg Ryan. Something about her smile drew Trevor in, and he couldn't stop looking at her.

"That gorgeous guy is looking at me," Carissa Dunn drawled to her friend Lara Abbott. She'd had several drinks, and her head was swimming in the warm, woozy land of weak inhibition and glee.

Lara stole a furtive look, then broke into an effusive smile. "Oh, Carissa!" she gushed. "That's Trevor Bullock. He's hot! He played baseball for the Huskers last year, and now he plays in the minor leagues with the Philadelphia Phillies."

"You mean you've met him and you never *told* me?" Carissa cried.

"Of course I've met Trevor Bullock. I write sports stories for the *Daily Nebraskan*, remember? He was one of the best pitchers we had!" Lara whispered excitedly. "If I let you know every time I met an athlete I'd be calling your cell phone every five minutes."

"It's just that he's so delicious! You really should have mentioned him."

Lara shrugged. "What difference does it make? C'mon; we'll talk to him now."

"Oh, yeah!" Carissa mouthed to Lara. Then leaning closer, she asked, "Did you say he plays for the Philadelphia Phillies?"

"No! He plays in the minor leagues for the Philadelphia Phillies *organization*!" Lara corrected.

"But *still* . . ." Carissa's eyes danced. "Someday he's going to be rich and famous!"

Lara rolled her eyes. "What*ever*, girl! You're so schnookered you'd probably trail behind any guy tonight!"

The girls slithered their way through the crowd and toward the bar, where Trevor and Aaron were casually imbibing frothy mugs of beer.

"Hello, Trevor," Lara said. "You probably don't remember me, but I'm Lara Abbott. I work for the *Daily Nebraskan*, and my friend here wanted to meet you."

Just then a 300-pound tank of a football player accosted the microphone: "Down with Missouri!" he bawled, while Joyce and her sidekick Paul began a lively little tune in jest of the luckless team that would be facing their beloved Cornhuskers the next day. The sound level increased 20 decibels as an army of Nebraska fans howled and cheered.

Trevor really hadn't heard Lara above all the excitement, but since she had that amazing blond in tow he smiled broadly and said, "Hey, how ya doin?"

Lara giggled nervously. "Oh, I'm doing fine."

"Who's your friend?" Trevor prodded.

"This is Carissa," Lara said, stepping aside.

Carissa smiled and swayed a bit into the bar.

"She just turned 21," Lara added as an explanation for her tipsy friend's obvious overindulgence.

Carissa blushed and tittered. Steadying herself, she gushed, "I hear you're a great pitcher or something. That's really awesome, I guess. I mean, since I came here to find a football player and everything, but now I've found you, and you're not a football player but that's OK with me, actually, because you're really gorgeous, and I told Lara she needed to introduce us, so she did, and I'm really glad. You know what I mean?"

Carissa had run out of air.

Trevor looked her up and down and liked what he saw. "Well, hey, girls, Aaron and I were just here checking things out and having a good time." He gave Aaron a sideways glance and popped him playfully in the belly as he spoke. "But I can't hear myself think in here! Would you two like to go someplace else with us? It sounds like the crowd is just getting started here."

The girls agreed, and the foursome snaked their way through the cream-and-scarlet throng and spilled out onto O Street, leaving the notes of "Mustang Sally" to be sung by others.

The street was alive with the throbbing sounds of night life pouring from bars and watering holes. The cool September air washed over Trevor, replacing the lingering feel of stagnant air that he suddenly realized he'd been breathing inside the club.

"So where shall we go?" Aaron asked. "I think Iguanas sounds good."

There was general agreement, and they made their way toward the neighborly feel of Iguanas. As they stepped through the door, Carissa grabbed Lara and pulled her toward the bathroom. "I gotta goooo!" she whispered to her friend.

Looking back over her shoulder, Lara held up a finger and motioned for the guys to wait.

"Come on, Trevor," Aaron said, pulling Trevor toward a corner table. "Let's sit down. What do you see in that girl? I mean, she is *wasted*. I thought you were done with that kind of girl after— What was that girl's name? Ashleigh? You know, the one your mom called 'Fluff.'"

Trevor snorted. "Oh, Carissa is nothing like Fluff!"

"Whatever you say, dude. I know how you love to date train wrecks!" He waved his hand in Trevor's face.

Batting Aaron's hand away, Trevor saw the girls coming out of the bathroom. He motioned to them and turned back to Aaron, who cocked his head and raised an eyebrow.

"So, have you girls always been friends, or what?" Trevor asked. "Aaron and me have been buds since junior high."

"And what a joy it's been!" Aaron quipped.

89

Giggling, Lara said, "We're sorority sisters."

"Well, that settles that!" Aaron blurted. "Come now, Trevor, let's go!" Aaron made as if he were getting up from the table.

"What are you talking about?" Trevor demanded, yanking Aaron back down into the chair.

Aaron leaned toward the girls and said in a stage whisper, "Trevor doesn't date sorority girls."

"I *might!*" Trevor responded. He really liked Carissa, and he wasn't about to cut the evening short.

"He doesn't date girls he meets in bars, either," Aaron continued in the same hushed tone.

"Would you just shut up!" Trevor whopped Aaron across the chest.

The problem was that Aaron had a point. Trevor had always made fun of the girls from Greek row, as well as people who hooked up in bars. But the walk through the crisp night air seemed to have revived Carissa, and she was beginning to make sense. He really wanted to get to know her.

"Hey, I know we just got here, but this sitting around and talking business isn't working for me," Trevor said. "Why don't we go dancing?"

"OK!" Lara bubbled.

"Yeah, that sounds fun to me, too!" Carissa seemed to be pretty much willing to go anywhere Trevor suggested.

Back out on O Street once more, they meandered toward Studio 14. Trevor and Carissa made sure they were walking together and hung back a little behind Aaron and Lara. Every now and then Aaron looked over his shoulder at the pair and shook his head. There was no denying that his pal Trevor was smitten.

After they had danced for a while, Aaron suggested that they all go to his apartment. It was getting late, and none of them felt like being out in the bustling pregame night any longer.

"You're an amazing dancer!" Carissa exclaimed as they settled onto Aaron's couch. "You must have some Africa-American blood in you, because I've never met a White guy who could dance like that!" She gave him a playful jab.

"Oh, yeah! Trevor's got the moves!" Aaron hooted. "He's had a lot of practice with partying hard, haven't you, T-Bull?"

"Oh, not so much." Trevor wouldn't meet Aaron's eyes.

Aaron opened the fridge and scanned the contents. "Let's see . . . want some bean dip?" He held up a jar and grinned.

"Put that in the trash!" Trevor ordered. "It's probably left over from your Super Bowl party last February!"

"Nope; I got it just last week." Aaron pretended to be insulted. "And the Super Bowl was the end of January—don't you know anything?" He rolled his eyes and shook his head. "Since I don't have any chips, we'll forget about the bean dip," Aaron decided, throwing the jar back into the fridge. "I guess there's always beer. Anybody want some?"

Trevor and Carissa nodded.

The minutes slipped away as they lounged on the couch, sharing stories from their past. Aaron mentioned that he liked to play the guitar.

"Well, go get your guitar!" Carissa insisted. "I wanna hear."

"It's just regular guitar playing," Trevor replied, trying to blow off Aaron's ability and keep Carissa's attention on himself.

"So what? I like guitar." She looked at Aaron expectantly.

"Yeah, me too!" Lara added. "Go get your guitar. We'd really like to hear you play something."

Aaron sauntered to his bedroom to retrieve the guitar.

"It's not that big a deal," Trevor insisted. "I don't know why you think you want to hear him play so bad."

"And I don't know why you *care* so much if I want to hear him play," Carissa shot back.

Trevor shrugged and decided to keep his mouth shut.

Aaron reappeared and began playing songs from the Dave Matthews Band. Carissa leaned back and closed her eyes. The music seemed as if it were chipping away the rough edges of her day and setting her soul right again.

Trevor noticed her peace and enjoyment, and he *hated* the thought that Aaron was the one making her happy. He stood up abruptly and began pacing behind the couch. "I play the guitar too, you know," he announced.

"Oh? Let's hear you." Lara sounded doubtful.

Snatching the guitar from Aaron, Trevor put his fingers on the strings and tried to remember some chords. What was that song he used to play? Hoping it would all come back to him, he began to strum a little.

"You're *terrible!*" Lara scoffed.

"Yes, please stop," Carissa agreed, putting her fingers in her ears.

"No, wait—I can do this!"

"No, you can't!" Lara retorted. "I thought Aaron was really good, but you need to put that thing down *now!*"

Carissa sat in the corner of the couch, laughing. "You really are awful," she said. "I think I could listen to Aaron all night, but you really need to stick with dancing and pitching."

Casting the guitar aside, Trevor grunted in frustration. Why did the first girl he had really liked in a while have to like Aaron better? How was that possible? Flopping back down on the couch, Trevor avoided Carissa's gaze. He was ready to go home. He'd promised his mom that he would go to church in the morning. He stood up. "You girls want a ride back to your house?"

A few minutes later they pulled up to the sorority house. Still nursing his wounded pride, Trevor asked for Carissa's phone number. She smiled and scribbled the number on a scrap of paper from her purse.

"I'm sorry I made fun of your guitar playing," she apologized. "I'd like to have you call me sometime. It really was a lot of fun dancing with you." She touched his arm and slid out the passenger door and dashed up the steps of the house. She turned and waved before disappearing through the front door.

☆ ☆ ☆

In church the next morning Trevor could think of nothing except Carissa. Pastor Nelson might have been delivering his best sermon ever, but it wouldn't have penetrated Trevor's consciousness. He stood up automatically for hymns, knelt for prayer, and finally got up to leave without a clue about what had transpired during the service.

Once Duaine had shot an elbow into Trevor's ribs and whispered, a little too loudly, "You know, as captain of the narcotics unit I've seen a lot of glassy-eyed people in my day."

"Dad! I haven't done dope in years. Lay off!"

Duaine gave an amused little snort.

Ardyce leaned out and locked them both in a threatening glare. Trevor pasted on his most innocent look and shrugged. Duaine cleared his throat loudly and focused his attention to the front.

For a moment Trevor tried to listen to the pastor, but then he began to imagine how wonderful Carissa would look all dressed up for church. He wondered what she was doing right now. He wanted to see her again very soon and—

"We're leaving, Trevor! Care to join us?" Ardyce's amused voice yanked him back to the present. Ardyce and Duaine exchanged glances. Something was definitely up with Trevor.

Once home, Trevor went straight to his room. Retrieving the scrap of paper, he dialed Carissa's number and waited impatiently. He *really* wanted to go out with her tonight. She finally picked up.

"Hey, Carissa, this is Trevor . . . from last night. How's it goin' today?"

"Oh, I'm doing fine. Thanks for calling. This is a nice surprise!"

"Yeah, well, I just really enjoyed being with you last night, and I'd like to see you again tonight. Let's meet at 7:00 for dinner and then find some fun—"

"Wait, Trevor, I can't," Carissa interrupted. "I already have a date tonight."

"No, you don't— I mean, you do?" Trevor sounded totally mystified. This had never happened to him. Girls didn't turn him down. During all his daydreaming in church the thought had never crossed his mind even once that Carissa might have a date with somebody else, or that she wouldn't break the date to be with him.

"I'm really sorry, Trevor, but it's a thing I promised to do months ago," Carissa said. "My ex-boyfriend is in a frat, and they have this barn party. All the guys bring dates, and there's line dancing and other stuff. I promised him I'd go. You know, you can't do-si-do without a partner. I'm real sorry, Trevor."

Sorry? She was *sorry*? She was choosing her *ex*-boyfriend over *him*?

A hot and pounding wave of jealousy washed over him. Swallowing hard, he said, "Oh, well, that's OK. Maybe we could have dinner tomorrow night instead."

"Yeah, that would be great!" Carissa responded brightly. "Give me a call again tomorrow about 2:00. We can work out the details then."

"OK, I'll do that." Trevor's voice had lost its swagger.

"Thank you for calling me, Trevor," Carissa said. "I'll see you tomorrow."

"All right. 'Bye."

Trevor hung up the phone and flopped down on the bed. He stared up at the ceiling and wondered what he was going to do to pass the time until he could see Carissa again.

☆ ☆ ☆

"How does Applebee's sound?" Trevor asked as Carissa climbed into the car.

"Good. That sounds good," Carissa responded, giving him an encouraging smile.

"So how'd the line dancing go last night?" Trevor kept his tone casual, offhanded. Maybe he'd be able to make her think that her time with another guy was no big deal to him. Or maybe she'd like the fact that he cared. In truth, he was begging for information about whether he had anything to feel jealous about.

Carissa wasn't fooled. "Trevor, I had a nice time last night," she said evenly, "but I'm glad I'm out with you tonight."

"I'm glad too," he said.

Carissa gave him a sideways glance and smiled ruefully.

At Applebee's they sat near the bar and ordered drinks. Trevor was eager to learn about Carissa and asked a lot of questions. "I've told you that my mom is big into the Seventh-day Adventist Church, and I go with her sometimes. What about you? Do you go to church much?"

"Well, I was confirmed a Methodist when I was 12, but since then I've basically been a Chreaster."

"A what?" Trevor looked confused.

"A Chreaster. You know, I only go at Christmas and Easter. I'm a Chreaster."

"Oh!" Trevor laughed. "I had *no* idea what you were talking about."

"I know," Carissa giggled. "You should have seen the look on your face when I said that. It was like you were terrified that I was part of some weird cult or something."

"Well, you do know how to get a reaction out of me," Trevor admitted. "Listen, I just really like you a lot."

"I like you, too."

Trevor looked at her earnestly. "Well, what I'm trying to say is that I'd really like to think of you as my girlfriend. I hated that you were out with some other guy last night."

"I know you did." Carissa smiled knowingly. "I'd like to give it a shot too." She reached across the table and touched his hand. For a moment their eyes locked. Then Carissa leaned back. "But I have to tell you that I'm not the type to get really serious about relationships. My dad died in a construction accident when I was 12, and I've watched my mom go through two divorces. I'm not planning on getting married. I want to be independent—get a job and live on my own. I've dated a lot of guys; I just don't take it that seriously."

Trevor blinked a couple times. This beautiful girl in front of him could be so disarming. What was a guy to say to a girl who just said her dad died when she was 12? Gathering his wits, he gave her his most understanding smile. "I think I know what you're saying. And it's OK. You *should* reach for your personal goals; I know I am. Baseball is consuming!"

"Well, that's kind of what I mean." Carissa still had a serious look on her face. "I won't be tagging along after you when you're off playing baseball."

"That's fine." Trevor was doing his best to sound encouraging. "We'll just see what happens during the off-season, all right?"

Carissa nodded.

"So can I call you my girlfriend?" he asked again.

"Sure," Carissa said. "We'll see what happens."

☆ ☆ ☆

"I think I've had enough dancing for tonight," Trevor said, pulling Carissa down into the seat next to him. It was Friday night, and they were back at Studio 14.

"I'm feeling kind of tired," he admitted. "I went running and did some weights earlier today. It's not like any of that should have knocked me out, but I just don't feel like dancing anymore."

"It's all right. I'm feeling kind of tired too. I had a big test in one of my business marketing classes today." She sighed and rested her chin in her hands.

"Would you be willing to come to church with me tomorrow? I told my mom and dad I'd go with them. And I'd love to see you dressed up all nice," Trevor said with a sly grin.

"I can't believe you just said that!" Carissa gave him a playful little slap on the shoulder.

"Well, will you come?"

"I guess so." Carissa leaned in for a quick kiss. "Who am I kidding? I'd like to see you dressed up nice too."

Chapter 12

Trevor and Carissa dated throughout the off-season, while Trevor was home. Occasionally they went to church together at the College View Seventh-day Adventist Church in Lincoln.

Before Trevor left in March 2001 for spring training in Florida, he stopped by Carissa's sorority house to say goodbye.

"I have something for you." He fished in his pocket and pulled out a ring. "It's only a 'promise' ring," he said. "I want you to know that I promise to come back to you when the season is over in September." He slipped it on her finger. "I'm really going to miss you—I hate that we're going to be apart so long. But I'll call you every day. I want this to work. I really love you."

Trevor leaned toward Carissa for a kiss. They lingered a bit in their embrace and Carissa thought she might cry, but she hoped she wouldn't. She tried to tell herself it wasn't a big deal if things didn't work out for them during his time away, but it did matter to her. Trevor had found his way into her heart, and she was going to miss him.

When she arrived in Clearwater a month later to visit Trevor, they stayed together in a hotel. While Trevor was busy during the day, Carissa was able to relax and visit with her uncle, who lived in Tampa.

The morning after her arrival, as Trevor prepared to leave, Carissa looked up sleepily and smiled. "I'm really glad you're here," he said, reaching out to brush her cheek with his finger.

"Me too. I'm really glad too," Carissa murmured back. "I'm excited to see you in your baseball world. I've never really gotten to see you pitch. I'm looking forward to it." Her finger lazily traced the gold chain hanging around Trevor's neck from which his jersey number dangled beside a gold mitt with a baseball in it. "My handsome baseball player," she added with a playful smile.

97

Trevor kissed her and said, "They're probably going to keep me pretty busy this morning, but later this afternoon you can come by and see me practice pitching, OK?"

"Sure, that's fine. I need to go visit with my uncle anyway, and then maybe I'll just lie by the pool. I'll see you later this afternoon."

"I can't wait to see you later." He shut the door and walked down the hall with a little extra strut in his step.

☆ ☆ ☆

Carissa scanned the field at the Phillies' training camp. She spotted Trevor over in the bullpen and could just see him around the heads of some other girls who were watching him too.

She stepped up to the fence and waited for Trevor to notice her. When he did, she waved. He smiled and kept pitching. She was amazed at how focused he was. His upper teeth kind of bit down over his lower lip as he concentrated on putting the ball right where he wanted it. Actually, he was kind of scary looking when he got this intense, but she thought he was very handsome anyway. The other girls seemed to think so too. Carissa didn't let on, but in her mind she whispered, *He's mine!*

When he finished his practice pitches, he came out of the bullpen and walked over to her. "Hi!" he said, producing a big warm smile.

"Hi!" she giggled back. "You're kind of popular around here."

"I guess so," he said sheepishly and led Carissa away from the other girls. "You wanna get dinner someplace?"

As they walked to the car, Carissa remarked, "I've seen a lot of strip clubs around here. Do a lot of the guys go?"

"Oh, yeah! The guys go." Trevor knew what the next question was bound to be, and he didn't care to field it. He went to the strip clubs too, but he didn't want to have that conversation with Carissa right now. "Hey, listen," he said quickly, "I want to take you someplace special. How about we go over to Tampa and just leave this place behind for a bit?"

The next day as Carissa lounged by the hotel pool a shadow passed across her face and stopped. Opening her eyes, she saw some guy she didn't know wearing a Phillies organization T-shirt.

"Hey!" he said. "Are you new around here? I didn't see you last year."

Caught a little off guard, Carissa stammered, "I'm just visiting someone."

"Well, would you like to visit with me for right now? My name is Lance. Maybe I could show you around the party scene of Clearwater." He reached down to take her arm.

"No!" Carissa jumped up, wrapping her towel around herself. "I'm here *with* someone!" She retreated to her room. This baseball world that Trevor lived in was unnerving! She would never say it (and was only just beginning to think it), but she was beginning to wish Trevor was still in Nebraska.

☆ ☆ ☆

After spring training Trevor was assigned to play with the Class A BlueClaws in Lakewood, New Jersey. It was the first year for the BlueClaws, and the team played before sellout crowds of more than 6,500 fans in beautiful, brand-new FirstEnergy Park.

Trevor rented a house in Lakewood with teammate Matt Riethmaier. Coming in after the first home game, they were exhausted yet jubilant.

"This place is amazing," Matt groaned happily.

Trevor couldn't agree more. "I know! I think I signed about 200 autographs—and I haven't even played yet!"

"You weren't short on attention from the dugout girls, either," Matt laughed. "Man, you walk into a bar or onto the side of the field, and you have your pick of the litter. How many phone numbers did you get tonight?"

"Oh, some." He hadn't told any of the girls that he had a girlfriend. A slight twinge of guilt poked at him, but he brushed it away quickly. He loved the limelight. It was cool getting all this attention. And these same girls were going to be at all the games. He deserved to enjoy them.

All the same, he decided to give Carissa a call. He stepped out of the house and dialed her number.

"Hello?" The voice on the other end sounded groggy.

"Hi, Carissa! It's me—Trevor."

"Trevor! I have to work tomorrow at the bank. I'm trying to sleep." She rolled over and looked at the clock. "Where have you been, Trevor? It's midnight your time! Are you drunk?"

"Yeah, I'm a little drunk," Trevor conceded, "but let me tell you about Lakewood. The fans here are awesome, and it's not far from Atlantic City—"

"Atlantic City? Did you go to Atlantic City *tonight?* Is that why you're calling me so late? Who are you with?"

"My roommate, Matt."

"Well, whatever, Trevor. I don't really care. I want to go to sleep. Don't call so late!"

The phone went dead in Trevor's hand. "Well, whatever yourself," Trevor snorted irritably. Maybe he *would* call one of the girls he'd met tonight. Maybe she'd listen to how excited he was to be here.

☆ ☆ ☆

"Fans, hit the floor!" the announcer boomed as Trevor loped out to the mound to toss a few warm-up pitches. The stadium erupted as thousands of feet began stomping and a swell of voices chanted, "Bul-LOCK! Bul-LOCK! Bul-LOCK!"

Duaine thought his chest was going to burst with pride. The place was coming undone for *his* son. Trevor was the BlueClaws' closer. He had secured the team's first home win by pitching five scoreless innings of relief against the Hickory Crawdads. He hadn't given up a run in the next game either. The Lakewood fans loved him.

Buster, the fuzzy yellow BlueClaws mascot, cavorted around in the left-field stands, his shaggy green mop of frizzy hair jiggling merrily atop his head. Expectations were high, and Trevor seemed to draw his very life's energy from the frenzied crowd. Winding up for the pitch, he delivered a two-seam fastball tight inside over the plate.

"Steee-RIKE!" The umpire bellowed, and Buster punched the air and danced.

Duaine hadn't had so much fun in a long time. Trevor was knocking out the batters one at a time, and the euphoria of the moment surrounded him with reassuring affirmation. All his dreams for Trevor were happening right before his eyes. The sky was the limit for his son!

When they met after the game, Duaine said, "That was great seeing you pitch like that!"

"Yeah!" Trevor grinned. "There's nothing like hearing the crowd call for you."

Eager young fans, sporting the BlueClaws crab logo on hats and T-shirts, began milling around, and Trevor signed whatever was handed to him.

"You've got some different stuff you're throwing," Duaine commented.

"Yup!" Trevor nodded. "Coach Nichols is really helping me; he's teaching me a forkball."

"Well, I know you'll throw any pitch at any time just to keep the batter off balance," Duaine boasted.

"You're right!" Trevor agreed. "Have you heard them call me a crafty left-hander yet? I kind of like hearing that." He smiled broadly.

"I like that one, too," Duaine agreed, patting Trevor on the back. "You keep up this kind of pitching, and you'll be in the big time before you know it! Everything is happening right for you."

But was everything happing right? He hadn't had a long talk with Carissa in days, and he missed her. Ardyce had just sent him another Max Lucado book, *The Applause of Heaven*, but he hadn't even cracked it open yet. He had to admit that he wondered if he might feel a little better if he were hearing the applause of heaven instead of the applause of Lakewood, New Jersey. His arm hurt, and he didn't like the feeling that any day on the mound could be his last. He was always one injury or a couple bad appearances away from being sent home. Then the fans would move on. They were fickle. But God wasn't fickle. He was pretty sure about that. Maybe he'd start reading that book. Maybe he'd really like to hear the applause of heaven.

Trevor Bullock Photo Album

Ardyce Bullock Photo Collection

LEFT: A 4-year-old Trevor stands beside his baby picture, showing off his new suit, circa 1981.

BELOW: Trevor, age 10, in the fifth grade (1987).

Ardyce Bullock Photo Collection

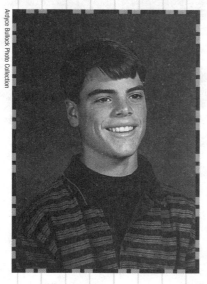

Ardyce Bullock Photo Collection

Eighth-grade picture, 1990-1991 school year.

ABOVE: Worlds of Fun, Kansas City, Missouri (1991).
From left: Aaron Madsen, Andy Wilcox, and Trevor Bullock.

BELOW: Lincoln Southeast High School Junior Homecoming,
1993. From left: Kit Minks, Trevor Bullock, Kurt Messenger,
and Chance Hanshaw.

ABOVE: Trevor displays his
Lincoln Southeast High
School Knights football
uniform, junior year
(August 1993).

Lincoln Southeast High School Christmas Ball, 1993. From left: Aaron Madsen and his date, Katie Vigna; Laurie Seward; Trevor's date, and Trevor Bullock.

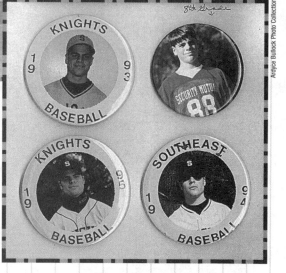

Sports buttons from Trevor's teenage sports days. Clockwise, from top left: Lincoln Southeast High School Knights (1993), eighth-grade football photo (1991), Lincoln Southeast High School Knights (1994), Lincoln Southeast High School Knights (1995).

BELOW: Trevor displays his Lincoln Southeast High School letterman jacket and some of his baseball uniforms (1995).

ABOVE: Trevor hams it up with his parents, Ardyce and Duaine, after his Lincoln Southeast High School graduation.

RIGHT: Trevor Bullock and Aaron Madsen (1995).

BELOW: Trevor and cousin Nate Lueders show off their high school diplomas (1995).

Brushed Back

RIGHT:
Trevor throws a pitch for the FirsTier Bank Youth Legion baseball team (1995).

BELOW:
Freshman year at the University of Nebraska at Kearney (1996). Trevor injured his pitching arm early in his freshman season.

Pastor Jeff Deming says a few words before Trevor's baptism (1997).

Ardyce Bullock Photo Collection

LEFT: Trevor delivers a pitch for the University of Nebraska (2000). Duaine Bullock's favorite picture of his son.

Ardyce Bullock Photo Collection

ABOVE: Trevor hurls a pitch in the first inning for the Beatrice Bruins, the elite college select team (2000). His pitching exploits for the Bruins, which included a five-inning no-hitter, helped the left-handed pitcher to walk-on and play for the University of Nebraska in the fall of 2000.

Trevor Bullock Photo Collection

Aaron Madsen, right, playfully hugs Trevor at a wedding celebration (2000).

Trevor Bullock Photo Collection.

LEFT: Trevor and Carissa at the 2001 spring training in Clearwater, Florida.

Trevor Bullock Photo Collection.

BELOW: Trevor pauses between signing autographs for the Lakewood, New Jersey, BlueClaws fans. The right sleeve of his uniform includes the logo for the Philadelphia Phillies, the BlueClaws' Major League Baseball parent club (2001).

Being on the road and staying in hotels takes its toll (2001).

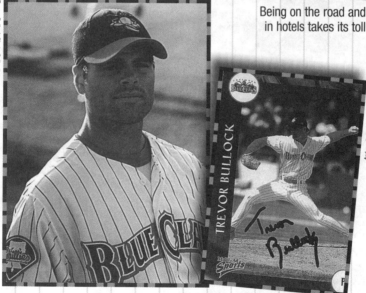

Trevor Bullock Photo Collection.

Ardyce Bullock Photo Collection

TREVOR BULLOCK

Trevor's 2001 Multi-Ad Sports baseball card for the Lakewood BlueClaws, which includes his signature. The back of the card features career highlights, 2000 season statistics, and biographical information.

LEFT: Carissa visits Trevor at the Lexington, Kentucky, stadium during the 2001 Lakewood BlueClaws season when she and Trevor's parents went to see Trevor pitch.

BELOW: Trevor and Carissa honeymoon in Cancun, Mexico (2002).

Trevor visits with Phyllis McMillen after giving his testimony at a Seventh-day Adventist church in Arizona (2002).

LEFT: Trevor and Carissa enjoy a vacation in Branson, Missouri (2004).

BELOW: Carissa, Duaine, and Ardyce Bullock during a vacation-birthday trip to Branson, Missouri (2004).

Trevor and Carissa with Pastor Jeff Deming in Oregon (2003). Deming baptized Trevor in 1997.

Trevor Bullock (2006).

Carissa Bullock (2006).

Carissa and Trevor, with Aaron and Bobbi Lee Madsen during a 2006 visit to San Francisco, California.

Trevor and Carissa relax with Drake (2004).

Chapter 13

"TierOne Bank. This is Carissa."

"Carissa! Where were you last night? I tried to call at least five times." Trevor's voice nearly shot out of the phone.

Glancing up briefly at the customer in front of her, Carissa put on her most professional voice. "Thank you for calling! I'm with a customer right now, but I'll be glad to call you back," she said sweetly.

Trevor was irritated. "Just forget it!" He wanted to be able to reach Carissa whenever he felt like it.

Chad Sadowski shot him a questioning look. Trevor and Chad had made a habit of rooming together when they were on the road. Both were pitchers, and it was nice to dissect the games with each other.

"She's working," Trevor answered glumly in response to Chad's unasked question. Trevor rubbed his arm and groaned. "My arm is really hurting."

"You say that a lot lately."

"Well, it hurts a lot!" Trevor crossed the room and picked up a container of Vaseline that he had doctored up with some kind of stuff vets put on horses' knees to help them recover after racing. It would have burned Trevor's arm if he had put it on straight, but once it was mixed with Vaseline it worked much better than IcyHot. He slathered the mixture on his arm, then flopped back on the bed. He decided to give Aaron a call.

"Hey, Aaron, this is Trevor."

"Oh, hey! What's up?" Aaron replied cheerfully. "How are the minor leagues treating you?"

"I'm doing all right. My arm's just a little sore, but this horse stuff I put on helps a lot."

"Horse stuff?" Aaron sounded a little confused. "Is it legal?"

"Oh, yeah; I think so. You know good and well that there are a lot of guys out here taking steroids and performance-enhancing stuff. It helps you recover faster. This is nothing compared to that."

"No, I suppose not," Aaron laughed. "But make sure you *don't* do that other stuff. You'll be dead by the time you're 40. Don't be one of those people who live for the moment. You have a future. You have Carissa and your parents—you have a lot of people who care about you."

"Yeah, Carissa . . ." Trevor said without enthusiasm.

"What's up, Trevor? Did something happen with Carissa?"

"No. Not really. She went to Vegas for spring break a couple weeks ago, but she told me nothing happened. I guess I just worry because I can't be there with her, and she's so beautiful."

"And does she need to be worried about you? You're pretty beautiful too!" Aaron teased.

"Oh, shut up, Aaron."

"OK. But seriously, do you love Carissa? Are you keeping yourself out of trouble?"

It was a question that only a very close friend could ask, and Aaron had asked it.

After a long pause, Trevor said, "I think I love her. I *must*. Otherwise, I would have moved on by now."

"So you're not spending time with any other girls out there?" Aaron couldn't hide the skepticism in his voice.

"Well—" Trevor hesitated.

"Trevor, you gotta stop messing around! What? Is it going to kill you to just march your tail back home after a game? Is there some reason you go off with the dugout girls and get drunk and gamble in Atlantic City?"

An ocean of guilt began to fill Trevor's belly. Aaron was right. Why couldn't he just do the right thing? Maybe if he came right home after a game he could call Carissa before she went to bed. "Aaron, I just don't know," he said finally. "I have to go out to eat after the games, and I just end up in the bar—I just do. The girls are there . . . They come over to me and flirt . . . Look, Aaron, I love Carissa, but I just can't control myself."

"All right, man, I understand." Aaron's tone had softened. "I remember in high school. Nate and I would drag you along to places just to get some girls to come around *us*." He laughed almost apologetically. "Nate called you the stink bait that brought the school of fish."

Trevor passed his hand over his eyes. "You know, Aaron, it's really hard playing in the minor leagues. When I first got to Clearwater for spring training the very first year I was feeling so proud of myself, and then I looked out at the field and there were hundreds of guys. They were all as good as me, and they all thought they were going to make it to the majors."

"Yeah, I know. I remember you telling me that."

"Every day I'm here I'm always hoping somebody higher up is going to be impressed," Trevor admitted. "And every night after a game I feel like I deserve a little pleasure for all my hard work."

"I can understand that." Aaron's voice was kind. "But Trevor, you just don't sound very happy."

☆ ☆ ☆

"TierOne Bank. This is Carissa!"

"Carissa! This is Ardyce Bullock." Trevor's mom sounded warm and friendly. "How are you doing today?"

"Oh, I'm all right." Carissa tried to sound genuinely peaceful. It wouldn't do any good to admit that she'd just gotten a clipped call from Trevor that made her feel sad somehow.

"I was wondering if you'd come to church with us this Saturday."

"Sure, yeah. I'll do that," Carissa heard herself say.

"Oh, good! It will be so nice to see you."

Carissa could hear the joy in Ardyce's voice. As she hung up she shook her head a little. Why had she just agreed to that? What was she thinking? *Oh, well,* she told herself, *at least I like the sermons that that Greg Nelson guy preaches."*

☆ ☆ ☆

"Arrrgggh! What have I done?" Chad sat on the edge of the bed holding his face in his hands.

"Are you OK?" Trevor rolled over in bed. "It's 4:00 in the morning, pal!"

"I know," Chad moaned.

"Did you just get in? Where have you been this whole time?" Trevor was shocked.

"Well, you know I pitched a pretty good game last night and—Ohhhhh . . . I can't even say it!" He toppled over and buried his face in his pillow.

"Can't say what? What'd you do?" Trevor couldn't imagine that Chad could have possibly done anything too terrible.

"There was a girl, Trevor." Chad refused to look up.

"You went with a girl? But you've been in love with Amy since high school!" This was impossible!

"I knooooooow!" Chad sounded as if he were crying.

Trevor sat up and thought he might pass out. He had drunk way too much himself. He turned on a lamp and swerved over to the sink to splash some cold water on his face. Then he turned to face his friend. "Look, Chad, this could have happened to anybody. The girls just throw themselves at us."

"I knooooooow!" Chad seemed absolutely bereft. He sat up suddenly and stared at Trevor. A passionate fire blazed in his eyes. "I know they throw themselves at us, but that's no excuse!"

Trevor was sort of hoping it *was* a good excuse, but Chad's intensity silenced any argument he might have tried to make.

"We have got to stop living our lives this way!" Chad cried fervently. "You know me; I was raised Catholic, and I went to church only for confession when I did something bad. But it never changed my heart. I need my heart to change, Trevor! Don't you think that if Jesus is really the savior of the world He ought to be able to change my heart?"

Trevor rocked back a little and sat down on his own bed. Hadn't his mother always told him that being a Christian—truly being a Christian—meant that you lived a new life with a changed heart? How long had he been making excuses that God knew his heart when all along God was trying to *change* his heart? "I don't know, man. What you're saying sounds about right," he finally managed to say.

Pulling out the Gideon Bible from the drawer by the bed, Chad declared, "I'm going to read about Jesus, Trevor. We've got to get to know Jesus. I love Amy so much, and I know you love Carissa. We can't keep living this way. We just can't!"

Gulping a little, Trevor flopped back onto his pillow. His head was pounding, and so was his heart. Chad was right. He needed to get to know Jesus.

☆ ☆ ☆

The ringing of the phone sounded far away. Carissa sat up and wondered for a moment where she was and what she was supposed to do about that dreadful sound in her ears. Her pulse quickened as she picked up the receiver and forced her voice not to shake.

"Hello?" It was as much a question as a statement.

"Carissa! This is Ardyce Bullock. I wanted to remind you about coming to church this morning."

"Oh, yeah! Thanks for reminding me."

"See you soon!" Ardyce sounded far too cheerful.

Carissa slumped back down in bed. "Oh, man!" she groaned. The room was swirling, and she thought she might vomit. "I have got the *worst* hangover ever!"

An hour later, after a pounding shower and a good strong cup of coffee, she applied her makeup and hoped it adequately covered the circles under her eyes. Slipping into a comfortable spring dress, she checked herself in the mirror and muttered, "Here goes."

Seeing Ardyce in front of the church, Carissa waved, and Ardyce hurried over and gave her a hug. "I know you went to the NextAdventure Sabbath school class with Trevor when you came last time, but let me actually introduce you to Shannon Minnick."

Carissa didn't actually want to be introduced to anybody, but Ardyce was so confident that this was a good thing she decided she wouldn't expend energy for much more than basic survival. It's not like she was going to argue. She still felt a little woozy.

"This is Shannon," Ardyce said, as she presented a kind-looking woman in a lavender linen dress. "Shannon is one of our associate pastors."

The two exchanged greetings, and Shannon directed Carissa to a place in the NextAdventure class. "I remember seeing you before. Are you very familiar with Seventh-day Adventists?"

"No, not really," Carissa admitted.

"Well, then, feel free to just listen in our class today. We'll answer any questions you have. I'm glad you're here." Shannon smiled warmly and went to greet another person coming into the class.

Carissa planned on sitting really still. The swirling in her head was bound to get better sometime soon. She hoped.

As she listened, the group shared prayer requests and prayed for each other. Then they began discussing Matthew 18:10-13. Shannon stepped over to Carissa and handed her a Bible. As the group discussed how Jesus is the shepherd who leaves the 99 sheep to go in search of the one that is lost, Carissa's heart was moved. Was it possible that she was like a lost sheep? Was she so caught up in going her own way that it wouldn't matter how hard she tried to make things right on her own? She had often felt powerless to change her situation, but if Jesus was the shepherd who was out looking for His sheep, maybe He was looking for her right now. She liked that thought.

"Would you like to study the Bible with me?" Shannon was standing beside her again. The class was over.

"Yes, I would," Carissa responded.

"Our women's group meets to study the Bible on Tuesday nights. We'd love to have you come. It's a much smaller group than what you saw today."

"Thank you. That sounds really good." Carissa couldn't believe how nice this group was. She had never been with a group of young adults who weren't three sheets to the wind or working on getting there. The difference was compelling.

☆ ☆ ☆

Trevor's amazing relief pitching streak continued. He still hadn't given up an earned run.

"I've never been a closer before, but every time I come out of the bullpen I shut the door!" Trevor beamed as he spoke to Chad.

"Yeah, Trevor; you're doing great."

Chad was clearly distracted. They were on the team bus on an unbearably long trip to play the West Virginia Power. Trevor was filling the time reading Max Lucado's *He Still Moves Stones* and listening to a Ray Boltz CD his mom had sent him. Beside him Chad was devouring the Bible.

Trevor's back felt stiff, so he stood up in the aisle to stretch. The ache in his neck was probably from reading so much, he thought, and his arm was throbbing. "I am getting so tired of being on this ———— bus!" Trevor complained.

Catcher Rob Avila shot out of his seat and fixed Trevor in a penetrating glare. "I don't ever want to hear you talking like that!" Rob was one of the Christian friends Trevor had begun studying the Bible with.

Lowering his eyes a little, Trevor mumbled, "I'm sorry. You're right."

"We're all trying to change our lives here," Rob continued. "We have to *act* as though being a Christian matters."

"Trevor, it's the little things that people notice," Chad added. "Being like Jesus needs to define you so that others can see that you love Him."

Trevor nodded. The guys were right. But frankly, the temptations in his life were still stronger than his fledgling faith. Although he loved God, so far he hadn't stopped drinking and gambling. And he loved Carissa, too, but he still had the phone numbers for the dugout girls in West Virginia saved on his cell phone.

☆ ☆ ☆

"Hey, Trevor, I'm starting Bible studies with Shannon Minnick," Carissa announced.

"You're doing *what* with *who*?" Trevor wasn't sure he was hearing things right. Was his cell phone breaking up? Maybe she said she was doing "libel studies." Maybe working in the business world required a better understanding of libel. That would make sense.

"I'm doing *Bible* studies!" Carissa repeated. "I'm going to stop drinking, Trevor. I really need to turn my life around."

"*You? Stop drinking?*" Trevor had thrown his head back for a hearty laugh. "I'm sorry, Carissa, but I'm not sure I can see that happening."

"I'm going to try, Trevor," she said with determination. "I'm beginning to think being a Christian is about having a relationship with God, and it's hard to get to know somebody when your head hurts all the time."

"OK, Carissa. Well, I hope that works out for you." Trevor ended the call and shook his head in amusement. He was positive that whatever it was that had gotten into Carissa was temporary at best.

Chapter 13

Dude! I could be that fat, fuzzy guy!" Nate had just spotted Buster, the team mascot, romping over by the bullpen. He was pretending that Trevor's left arm was burning him every time he touched it. "Look! I can dance!" Nate popped out of his seat and began bouncing about in an animated fashion. "I just looooove blue crabs from the Joysey shore!" he chortled.

"Would you shut up and sit down?" Aaron grabbed Nate and pulled him down. "They're called blue-*claw* crabs," he corrected. "And I'm trying to enjoy the game here! It looks like they're about to put Trevor in."

The BlueClaws had just scored six runs in the bottom of the eighth inning to take the lead over the Hagerstown Suns. Trevor was coming in at the top of the ninth to seal the deal.

"Fans hit the floor!" the announcer ordered. Immediately the stadium exploded into a thundering, stomping madness: "Bul-LOCK! Bul-LOCK! Bul-LOCK!"

"Oooooh, this is *exciting*!" Nate gasped, pretending to swoon.

Aaron rolled his eyes. Nate was incorrigible.

After the game Aaron and Nate waited for Trevor outside the locker room. Trevor signed autographs for a while, then sauntered over. "Hey, guys! What's up? Did you enjoy the game?"

Moving in close to Trevor, Nate pretended to be a dugout girl, "Ooooh, Trevor, I sure did enjoy the game!" he chirped in a high falsetto. "But not as much as you're going to enjoy the game I have waiting for you tonight!"

"Get off me, you big moose!" Trevor shoved Nate away and looked over at Aaron. "Would you like to go grab some dinner with me?"

"Naw! We're not hungry. We ate during the whole game," Aaron said. "We really need to get to bed, because we've got to travel back to Lincoln tomorrow."

"Yeah!" Nate agreed, letting out a long, loud belch. "We already ate."

"Well, I'm glad you came," Trevor said, giving them both a slap on the back.

☆ ☆ ☆

Trevor was on another long bus ride to play the Delmarva Shorebirds. He was feeling reflective, and wanted to talk to Carissa. After Aaron and Nate left the ball park, Trevor had gone to a strip club. Now he was sitting on the bus reading from the book of Romans in the Bible and feeling as though victory over sin was beyond his grasp and not at all the way Paul portrayed it in Romans. He felt terrible that he hadn't spent more time with the guys, and even more terrible that the time he could have been spending with them was spent instead with some nameless girl in a crowd of intoxicated revelers.

He dialed Carissa's number. When she heard his voice, she said, "Trevor, we need to talk. I've been really studying with the women's group, and I want to know if you and I are on the same page. I know you've been studying with some of the guys you're with, and I think we need Jesus to be part of our relationship."

Trevor groaned inwardly. He thought Carissa was probably right about Jesus being a part of their relationship, but even though he was reading the Bible and hoping to lead a Christian life, there were so many things he couldn't resist. It just didn't seem fair to drag Carissa along on his limping journey. He sighed. "I'm just not there yet, Carissa. I'm sorry, but I'm just not keeping my promises to you."

"But I love you, Trevor." Carissa had started crying. She was finding it hard to give up many of her habits, too, and if Trevor wasn't willing to give them up with her, how could she hope to succeed? She had shared these very thoughts with the others in the women's group. They had encouraged her to be strong in her own life and leave behind the things—*all* the things—that were holding her back. "I think we need to break up, Trevor." She forced the words out in spite of her sobs. "I think I need to try to put my life together all on my own with the support of the friends I have here."

"You're probably right," Trevor said quietly.

The call ended, and Trevor stared out the bus window. So that was it. He forced on a mask of bravado, but inside his thoughts tumbled wildly. Suddenly he wanted to talk to his friend.

"Hey, Aaron! I'm sorry I missed talking to you more after the game."

"It's all right, man." Aaron crossed the room and settled into his favorite chair.

"I'm just getting so tired of this . . . Carissa and I just broke up," Trevor admitted. "But it's not just that. I'm tired of playing minor league ball. I'm tired of the bus rides. I'm tired of being away from home. I know you think I'm crazy for saying it, but I miss my mom."

Aaron laughed. He couldn't help himself. "I know you miss your mom, dude. You've always been a mama's boy. But just remember, you are living the dream. We all dreamed of getting where you are now. Nate and I were so jealous when that stadium let loose cheering for you!"

"It's not as great as it seems," Trevor responded darkly. "I mean, when it's happening, it's great, real great, and I can't get enough. All that noise just makes me strut on the mound. But then when everything gets quiet, and I'm stuck on this stupid bus for another stupid five hours, I just don't think I can take it anymore. I love Carissa—how could I screw this up so much?"

"It'll be OK." Aaron tried to sound encouraging. "You have only a few more months, and then maybe you can patch things up with Carissa."

Trevor heaved a long sigh. "Maybe you're right. Thanks for coming to watch. It really did mean a lot to me."

Rob Avila slid into the seat next to Trevor. "You're looking a little lost."

"I just broke up with my girlfriend," Trevor said, turning to stare out the window again. "And you and the guys always talk about Jesus being stronger than our sin, but He's not, Rob! I'm telling you, He's not!"

Rob looked genuinely sad. "*You* are the one who's not bigger than sin, Trevor."

Trevor had half expected him to explode into some angry defense of God; instead he looked as if he were about to cry.

"I've watched you, Trevor," Rob continued. "You're the man. You control the ball game. You can put a pitch anywhere you want. You're about the best pitcher I've ever gotten to catch for. You look down the line at the batter, and you've got confidence dripping out of your pores. But off the field you can't control anything. It's *you* who can't control sin, Trevor."

Trevor nodded.

"God is like the perfect catcher," Rob continued. "If you go with the pitches He calls, you will never lose control of the game of life. Your sins will be knocked off like a batter who just can't get a piece of the ball. But the minute you start thinking that His calls are too hard for you to pitch or too stupid for you to try, the minute you start shaking Him off and going with your own pitches, the game is over. God is the perfect catcher, Trevor. You gotta start going with the pitches He calls." He handed Trevor a CD. "Listen to this. I think you might like it."

"Thanks," Trevor mumbled, rubbing his forehead. He watched Rob walk back to his seat. He wasn't sure he agreed with Rob about God being like a catcher. Most of the catchers he'd known had charged out to the mound when he shook them off. You could always count on a catcher to rip into you when you failed to give him what he wanted. Trevor didn't like thinking of God being a catcher, even a perfect catcher. And he was certain that any kind of God who wouldn't help him keep Carissa wasn't worth pitching for anyway.

Glancing down, he read the name on the CD: *Third Day.** Trevor put on his headphones and began to listen, surprised when the music started. It was a hard rock sound, nothing like the Christian music he'd heard previously. It penetrated his soul. As some of the lyrics began to sink into his mind, he felt his anger toward God soften, replaced by a renewed willingness to give God another chance—another chance for this God who had pursued him so tirelessly with His love, with His whispered words of forgiveness.

☆ ☆ ☆

"O Lord!" Carissa cried. "Help me, please; help me know what to do."

Thinking of Trevor was a habit. No matter how hard she tried to put thoughts of him out of her mind, she still had them. She wondered what he'd say about this, or wondered what he thought of that. She remembered how bonded she'd felt with him. Her feelings were so incredibly overwhelming, and they weren't going away.

She shared with the women's group that they had broken up. Everybody was supportive and encouraged her, saying that she had done the right thing, but it just didn't *feel* right. If this was so right, then how come she was still tossing and turning in the silent emptiness of the night? Why did the desire to call Trevor make her feel as if her throat were going to constrict all the way shut? Why was she still crying five times a day? Wasn't God supposed to give you peace when you made a decision for Him? One thing Carissa knew: there was no way to describe her feelings as peaceful.

☆ ☆ ☆

"Now entering the game for the Lakewood BlueClaws—pitcher Trevor Bullock!" The announcer's voice echoed around Applebee's Park as Trevor ran out onto the mound to pitch the final inning against the Lexington Legends. He wiped a little sweat from his forehead before settling in on the mound. Looking in for the pitch, Rob signaled a slider. Trevor didn't agree and shook him off. Maybe Rob had forgotten exactly where his slider came in. Then Rob signaled a four-seam fastball, and Trevor liked it. He was pretty sure he could get the ball to sail right in for a strike. After a couple fastballs he thought a changeup would do the trick and retire the batter, one, two, three.

Trevor turned his back and sailed out of his windup, delivering a heater straight in over the plate. With a familiar *thwack*, Mike Hill nailed the ball for a solo home run. Trevor knew it, and so did Rob. They didn't even have to see the ball sail over the fence; it just *sounded* like a home run. It was Trevor's fourth earned run in three days.

Rob trotted out to the mound and gave Trevor a fierce look. "I've been calling this game all day. What makes you think you can come running in here and shake me off?"

Trevor had no intention of being messed with. "I thought—"

"That's the problem! You thought!" Rob retorted. "You've got to just trust me!" Stepping closer, he said, "This is what I'm talking about with God. You've got to just trust Him. You can't keep thinking you know better than He does."

"We're losing 10 to 2!" Trevor snapped. "I wouldn't be real proud of calling this game, if I were you! And you're *not* God, so I'll shake you off if I want to!"

Rob smirked and walked back to the plate. He'd heard that Trevor pitched better when he was mad. And maybe a seed had been planted in Trevor's mind in the process. It's important to keep trusting God even when it *looks* as though He's got it all wrong.

Trevor hurried back to his hotel room after the game. For the past couple weeks he'd successfully blown off the dugout girls with vague excuses and joined Chad in catching a quick meal before retiring to the room to read. He turned to Psalm 121: *"I lift up my eyes to the hills—where does my help come from? My help comes from the Lord, the Maker of heaven and earth"* (verses 1, 2).

As the team drove around the countryside in the bus, Trevor had lifted his eyes to a fair number of hills, as well as every other kind of terrain imaginable. He'd been doing a lot of praying and felt as if his help truly *had* come from the Lord. If he'd been able to keep himself away from the destructive lifestyle, maybe he could promise Carissa that he'd changed. Picking up his phone, he dialed her number.

"Carissa, I think I can do it. I think I can change and make things work for us. I don't want to lose you. I love you!"

Carissa collapsed into happy tears. "I love you, too! I want to make things work too!"

"We need to pray," Trevor said. It was kind of weird praying over the phone, but Trevor was determined to do as Carissa had asked and put Jesus in their relationship.

After asking God to guide them, Carissa said, "Trevor, your parents are planning a trip to Lexington later this month to watch you play, and they invited me to come along. I'm going to come. I feel awful without you and hope that seeing you will help us get closer again."

"That sounds great!" Trevor said. "I want to see you too."

When he finished telling Carissa about the past few weeks and the things he'd been reading, Trevor said good night and ended the call with a heartfelt "I love you." As he rolled off the bed to put his phone on the desk, he caught sight of Chad and stopped. Chad's eyes were pools of tears, and his face was radiant.

"What's the matter with you?" Trevor asked.

"Nothing." Chad swiped at his eyes with his arm. "I guess I'm just a sucker for love."

"Oh, you *are* pathetic!" Trevor laughed. "If I'm not crying, why are you?"

"I'm happy for you," Chad said. "Now let me have my moment."

Trevor set the phone down and returned to his bed. "Thank You, Lord," he whispered. Even if he wasn't crying, he felt pretty relieved to have Carissa back in his life.

★ *Third Day, Offerings: A Worship Album,* "King of Glory."

Chapter 14

Unfolding herself out of the Bullocks' car, Carissa looked around Applebee's Park, home of the Lexington Legends. They'd been driving nearly 13 hours, and she was eager to see Trevor. She entered the stadium and ran along the concourse until she reached the right-field side, where Trevor would be warming up in the bullpen. Scampering down the steps, she leaned over the fence and spotted him.

"Trevor! Trevor!" she called, waving her hand wildly. She had pictured this moment in her mind for days. She imagined leaning over the fence and wrapping her arms around his neck. He would be so happy to see her! "Trevor!" she called again.

He looked up, straight at her, and nodded. Then he looked back at the guy who was catching and threw another pitch.

"He kind of takes pitching seriously," Ardyce said sympathetically, coming up behind Carissa. "We'll be able to have a better visit with him after the game."

As the game got under way, Carissa tried to shake off her disappointment at Trevor's cold response. The air was electric with the upbeat excitement of a minor league game. Big L, the Legends bigheaded baseball player mascot, and his equally bigheaded wife, Elly, were mingling with the squealing children who ran to them for hugs and a chance to goof around. The smells of popcorn, hot dogs, and beer swirled around in the air with the lively music.

Carissa could see Trevor sitting in the bullpen. She thought he was watching her, too, but it was a little hard to tell. Maybe he *was* glad to see her!

The game was close, but the BlueClaws were trailing. Trevor stood up and began warming up. He sure did have a swagger. Watching his command of the ball and the power that exploded out through his arm with every pitch, Carissa felt a little tingly. That incredible guy out there was *her* boyfriend. It was a very thrilling thought.

When Trevor entered the game in the bottom of the eighth inning, the score was tied. Carissa watched in amazement as Trevor struck out all three batters to end the inning. It seemed as if he'd just gotten onto the mound, and he was already running off the field.

"Wow!" Carissa breathed, turning to a beaming Ardyce.

Duaine madly flipped through his list of stats. Trevor hadn't shown himself to be a strikeout pitcher with the BlueClaws. He usually struck out only one or two batters, but already he'd struck out three in a row. "He's doing really well!" Duaine announced. He wondered if it was because Carissa was here.

Coming back in the ninth inning, the score was still tied. Trevor flew into his windup and sent a curveball flying toward John Buck. "Strike!" the umpire barked, and Duaine let out his signature whistle. Trevor was on fire. He went on to strike out Buck and Mike Rosamond. The third out was a pop fly to right field by Brian Schmitt.

The game went into extra innings. In the top of the tenth, Derrick Lankford smacked a solo home run just inside the foul line to sail over the left-field fence, putting the BlueClaws in the lead.

"He's gonna get the win; he's gonna get the win!" Duaine shouted, bouncing with anticipation.

In the bottom of the tenth Trevor proceeded to strike out pinch hitter Fehlandt Lentini.

"He's struck out *six* batters!" Duaine chortled, nearly beside himself. This whole business of having his family here (or maybe it was just Carissa) was really making Trevor strut.

Then the magic seemed to slowly slip away. Felix Escalona grounded out to center field, leaving the BlueClaws only one out away from winning the game. Trevor's next pitch was pounded hard to center field by Tommy Whiteman. The ball bounced before reaching Jason Barnette. Jason caught it and threw, but it was too late, and Whiteman made it to first.

"Give him the dark one!" Ardyce hollered as the next batter came up.

Trevor delivered a two-seam fastball that wafted out and up before reaching catcher Daniel Tosca. The ump ruled it a ball.

"C'mon, Blue!" Ardyce thundered, nearly scaring Carissa out of her skin. This wasn't the kind, warm Ardyce she'd come to know!

Exploding out of the windup, Trevor threw a slider. The pitch came in over the plate, curving and rising slightly. German was ready. With a mighty swing he sent a screamer out to right field. Gregg Foster dove for the ball and snagged it with just the tip of his glove, scooping it in toward his body. The ball bounced around a little under his chest before he nabbed it and tossed it back to Trevor to hold the runners. Whiteman had advanced to third, and German was on first.

Manager Greg Legg jogged out to the mound to talk to Trevor. Carissa saw the two shaking their heads. Then Legg patted Trevor on the back and called in Eude Brito to retire Jon Topolski and sew up the game. The BlueClaws won 7 to 6.

☆ ☆ ☆

"That was wonderful!" Duaine was absolutely thrilled about Trevor's dominance in the game. "*Six* strikeouts! The most you've had before was four against the Charleston Riverdogs!" Duaine kept close track of these things.

Trevor smiled, looking over his dinner at Carissa. He had come out of the locker room after the game and given her a warm hug and kiss, but Carissa still felt he was slightly reserved in front of his teammates and parents. Perhaps that was all right. She had hoped to have some special time with him to rekindle the flame, but so far things had been forced into the more public, peripheral kinds of interactions.

Leaning in, she whispered, "Can I come by your room tonight? I'd like to spend some time with just you."

"No, you can't," Trevor told her apologetically. "Club rules forbid even wives to be in the rooms with the players."

Carissa was shocked. "But the players pick up girls from the community all the time! You can't tell me that all those girls who hang around the fence don't end up in the rooms!"

Trevor laughed and motioned for her to simmer down. "They do," he admitted, "but they aren't supposed to. And they have to sneak in and then sneak out before dawn."

129

Carissa wanted to say that she could sneak too, but she thought better of it in front of Trevor's parents. Maybe after the next game she could spend a few hours with him somewhere. Tonight she was too tired to push it.

☆ ☆ ☆

"It's 8:00!" Ardyce announced. "Time to get up!" she said, pulling Carissa from her warm nest of sleep.

In the other bed Duaine groaned. Ardyce might be thrilled it was Sabbath morning, but everybody else in the room was still working on their enthusiasm.

"I'm calling Trevor!" Ardyce proclaimed, dialing the number. "He needs to get up too. I've found a church, and Sabbath school starts at 9:30."

Duaine groaned again. Carissa forced her eyes to stay open. Of all the days that it might have been nice to skip church, this would be the one. But Ardyce had a plan, and Carissa knew better than to try to avoid it.

Later, as she sat next to Trevor in church, Carissa held his hand tight. She leaned slightly into him and felt the warmth of his sturdy build. He wore a nice suit and had gotten every hair in place. Everything about him was yummy, in her opinion. She knew he had to return to the stadium by 1:30, so she planned to stay as close to him as she could until then.

Duaine eyed the two of them and looked as if he were going to whisper some sort of obnoxious comment when Ardyce elbowed him hard. So instead he rolled his eyes and turned his attention back to the speaker. Trevor let go of Carissa's hand and smiled at his mother. Everyone was towing the line with Ardyce now.

Trevor didn't pitch at all during the next game. In fact, it was disappointing all the way around. Lakewood was shut out, losing 2-0.

Sunday morning was a chance for everybody to catch a little extra sleep. When she slithered out of bed around 11:00, Carissa felt refreshed. She and Trevor had gone to dinner the night before, and she'd hoped they might eat breakfast together too. Grabbing some shorts and a T-shirt, she slipped into the bathroom to get dressed. As she shut the door she heard Duaine suggest, "Let's go get breakfast at Cracker Barrel."

Steadying herself against the door, Carissa almost felt like crying. She'd just spent two nights in a hotel room with Trevor's parents and had had minimal time with Trevor. Maybe this hadn't been such a good idea. Taking a deep breath, she forced herself to smile. Cracker Barrel would be OK. And having a chance to watch Trevor in action had been worth the drive, she decided. He was amazing!

☆ ☆ ☆

Trevor watched the game from the bullpen. Lakewood and Lexington were locked in a 1-1 tie. He felt a little bad that he hadn't found a way to spend more time with just Carissa, but it was awkward having his parents here too. He was determined to find a moment to at least whisper in her ear how much he loved her, how fantastic she looked.

As he looked into the stands he saw Carissa get up and walk toward the exit and onto the stadium concourse. Just as she approached the exit, a guy hopped down beside her from the top seats. When he got close, she stopped briefly, then laughed. As she slid into the shadows, Trevor saw the guy reach out and gave her a friendly pinch. The rest was left to his imagination as they both rounded the corner and disappeared from sight.

Trevor felt sick. This proved it—Carissa couldn't be trusted! Swallowing his anger, he tried to focus on the game. First things first. But that guy better hope he didn't find him after the game.

In the bottom of the ninth inning Trevor was called in to pitch. Before getting his sign from Daniel, he looked into the stands one last time to make sure Carissa was safely squared away next to his mom. She was. He could see her cheering for him.

His first pitch was a two-seam fastball that moved away from Felix Escalona as he reached for the ball and missed.

"Strike!" the umpire bellowed.

Trevor was at it again. The two-seamer worked so well the first time that he and Daniel decided to try it again, and with the same result. Trevor's final pitch to Escalona was a changeup that lumbered into the plate, getting to Daniel's glove long after Escalona had swung.

"He's striking them out again!" Duaine's jubilation could not be contained.

Turning to face Tommy Whiteman, Trevor gave the two-seam fastball another try. Whiteman stepped into the plate and met the ball with a swinging bunt that dribbled back toward Trevor's feet. Trevor was taken by surprise and had to shift his weight to run up on the ball and pivot around to throw it to first. His throw wasn't in time. Whiteman made it on base.

Trevor drew his breath in sharply. *OK, focus,* he told himself. He heard his dad's familiar whistle in the mayhem of sounds floating out of the stands.

Ramon German stepped up to the plate and grounded out. Whiteman stayed on first. Jon Topolski came up next. Daniel signaled a split-finger fastball, and Trevor delivered the pitch.

"Strike!"

Next came a curveball, sailing wide over the outside corner of the plate. It was ruled a ball.

"C'mon, Blue!" It was Ardyce, but this time her intensity came as little surprise to Carissa.

Trevor delivered the same curveball, sending it a little farther inside. Topolski didn't swing, and the ump called a strike. The final pitch to Topolski was the forkball Trevor had been practicing. It came in the same way the split-finger fastball had, only slower. Topolski swung, and hit air.

Mike Hill entered the batter's box and swung on Trevor's first pitch, pelting the ball out to Gregg Foster in right field. The ball bounced once, and Gregg had to trap it against the outfield fence before turning to throw it in. Hill was safe at first, and Whiteman advanced to second.

Trevor stranded the runners when John Buck slapped the ball high behind the plate, and Daniel jumped up and caught it.

The score remained tied as Trevor came back in to pitch the bottom of the tenth inning. He struck out Mike Rosamond, then allowed two more hits before Manager Greg Legg pulled him out. Carissa felt sad as she watched Trevor leave the game. She was about to have to leave him again. The visit had been far too short.

The Lakewood BlueClaws and the Lexington Legends battled for a couple more innings before the Legends scored a single run in the thirteenth inning to win the game 2 to 1.

Carissa leaned against the rail and turned her face to soak up the sun. She anticipated having to wait at least a half hour before seeing Trevor emerge from the locker room. Closing her eyes, she ran her fingers through her hair and waited.

Suddenly Trevor was beside her. Sweat still glistened on his face. "Who was that guy you were with? What were you two doing?" he blurted angrily.

"What guy?" Carissa was completely baffled.

"The friend you met in the stands! You seemed kind of familiar with him. Who was he?"

"I didn't meet anybody," Carissa began, then the realization dawned. "Oh, you mean that totally drunk guy who pinched me?"

"Yes!" Trevor thundered. "Who was he? You obviously were enjoying it. I saw you laughing!"

"Calm down, Trevor!" Carissa stammered, trying to steady her own fluttering heart. "I didn't know him at all. He was just some random guy!"

"You were laughing with him!"

"No! I was laughing *at* him, Trevor!" Carissa was angry now herself. How many times had she turned the other way and pretended not to notice the dugout girls fawning over Trevor? At least a million. "He was just some stupid, ugly, oversauced baseball junky who couldn't even form a meaningful sentence!" she seethed. "I was laughing *at* him!"

"A likely story!" Trevor sniffed.

"It's true. And you wanna know what else is true? I don't believe all *your* pathetic stories about who you're with late at night!"

There. She'd said it. But in the saying of it she was brought up short. She had always tried hard not to overthink their separation, tried to give Trevor the benefit of the doubt. But now that she thought about it, what *was* he doing every night while she was waiting at home to hear from him? She turned away. "I've gotta go, Trevor," she said flatly.

All the fight seemed to go out of Trevor. The temptation to defend himself was strong, but he took a deep breath and said, "OK. I'll call you once you get home."

Carissa wanted to pull him into one last kiss goodbye, but it was already too late. He was walking over to say goodbye to his parents. She slipped past them and waited by the car. She was really hoping Trevor's mom and dad would leave her alone on the trip back. She was sure they'd seen the blowup.

Chapter 15

Trevor, wait up!" Chad ran to catch up with Trevor as he walked toward the team bus. "I wanted to remind you that you're leading the Bible study next week. It's on the Ten Commandments."

"Oh, yeah. Thanks for reminding me." Trevor settled into a seat and began to think about the Ten Commandments, trying to remember what the first commandment was. Something about God . . . or something. He'd probably have to study some more if he was going to know enough to lead the discussion.

Then his thoughts drifted to Carissa. It was strange, but after feeling as if God had given him the victory over some of his bad habits, he was beginning to want to go back to them. If Carissa believed he was cheating on her, then why not go ahead and do it? After all, he wasn't so sure about *her* loyalty anymore, either.

☆ ☆ ☆

"So how was everybody's week?" Shannon Minnick was getting things started in the women's Bible study group.

Carissa listened as some of the others shared the events of their ordinary week. She purposely held back. She knew they thought Trevor was bad for her. Why should she confirm it by sharing how he'd doubted her and attacked her for something over which she had no control?

"Carissa, you went to Kentucky this past weekend, didn't you, to see Trevor? How did that go?" Lisa Shafer wasn't going to let her off the hook.

"It was all right," Carissa said. "I really didn't get to see him that much, but it was fun watching the games."

Lisa exchanged glances with Cheryl Olson and Kendra Carlson. Carissa noticed and felt a little defeated. They knew something was wrong, and she knew they knew. But she didn't want to talk about it. Her mom had already begged her to move past Trevor. This group was bound to do the same. Their looks of pity only confirmed her feeling that they thought she was stupid for staying with him. *She* thought she was stupid too, but matters of the heart were never as simple as simply deciding that something was stupid. She still really wanted things to work with Trevor.

Carissa turned the pages in her new Bible and tried to listen as the others began discussing Romans 8:38 and 39. The Bible, a recent gift from Ardyce, felt fresh in her hands, the pages crisp as she turned them. She stared at the words as Shannon began reading:

"'*For I am convinced that neither death nor life, neither angels nor demons, neither the present nor the future, nor any powers, neither height nor depth, nor anything else in all creation, will be able to separate us from the love of God that is in Christ Jesus our Lord.*'"

Carissa began to cry. She felt an arm around her, and somebody handed her a tissue.

"I know you all think I'm crazy," she sputtered, "but I love Trevor so much. And it just seems as though it doesn't take much at all to separate me from his love. But the verse says that nothing can separate us from God's love . . . and I guess that just—" She took a shivery-sounding breath and continued, "I don't know; it just makes me want to cry because God loves me so much, but also because Trevor *doesn't*." The final words triggered a fresh river of tears as Carissa released all the hurt she had forced back over the long weekend of hoping for real intimacy with Trevor.

☆ ☆ ☆

Trevor stared at Exodus 20 and didn't even know how to begin. It seemed as though everything he read pierced his conscience somehow. Verses 2 and 3, for example:

"*I am the Lord your God. . . . You shall have no other gods before me.*"

If he really thought about it, he knew that "other gods" were things that meant more to a person than God. He'd always convinced himself that he really loved God, but he couldn't deny that he loved baseball quite a lot—in particular, his own left arm.

And then there was the matter of the fourth commandment in verses 8 to 11. How *did* he plan to bring up the subject of the Sabbath?

"Remember the Sabbath day by keeping it holy. Six days you shall labor and do all your work, but the seventh day is a Sabbath to the Lord your God. On it you shall not do any work."

He looked over at the calendar and hoped he could wiggle out of having to admit that Saturday was the Sabbath. But all anyone had to do was count the days in the order they appeared on the calendar and know there was no way to wiggle. Saturday was the seventh day, and it said right there in the Bible that the seventh day was the Sabbath. God asked us not to work on that day. Maybe the other guys wouldn't call him on it. Everybody knew he played ball on Saturday.

Suddenly Trevor wanted to talk to Carissa. He knew she was studying the Bible these days. Maybe she could understand his feelings of guilt. Maybe she could help him figure out what to say to the other guys.

"Carissa," he said when she answered, "can we talk? I'm struggling with some things."

Carissa felt like saying that she too was struggling with many things. She wished Trevor would apologize for flying off the handle at her. But he wasn't going to. Well, at least he was confiding in her. "What do you want to talk about?"

As Trevor began to share his thoughts and struggles, she was surprised that his conscience seemed to be really speaking to him.

"I feel as if my priorities are all wrong, and I'm just not sure what to do about it," Trevor admitted.

"Well, let's pray," Carissa said simply.

☆ ☆ ☆

"So you're saying you believe Saturday is the Sabbath?" Todd Meldahl asked.

"Uh, well, yeah, I do." Trevor searched his mind for a way to shift

137

the conversation from the subject of which day of the week was Sabbath. Wasn't it far better to get into a discussion of the importance of Sabbath rest, or some other more benign aspect of the Sabbath? Certainly all these guys could agree that *rest* was important. For sure, nothing had ever run Trevor as ragged as minor league baseball.

"But you don't keep Saturday holy," Scott Youngbauer pointed out.

They weren't going to let this go. "Well . . ." Trevor struggled to find the right words. "I keep it holy in my heart. I *remember* what day it is while I'm doing stuff. And I figure that if God made me this talented in baseball, then He must be proud that I'm having a great year, regardless of the fact that I'm pitching on Saturday sometimes."

Rob, Chad, Todd, and Scott exchanged questioning glances. They weren't convinced. Worse, Trevor knew he wasn't convincing himself.

☆ ☆ ☆

Carissa stared at the door of the bank. Her day was almost over, and the urge to lose herself in a drink or two was becoming stronger and stronger. Her hot-and-cold relationship with Trevor was getting so *old*. When he had called in a fit of conscience and they had prayed together, Carissa had actually thought something was changing with Trevor. But she hadn't heard from him since. Was he thinking of her? How could she know?

When she left the bank, Carissa went straight to O Street. Maybe she'd give Sidetrack a try. Maybe if she stopped off in there she could find the elusive spark that had first brought her to Trevor.

The atmosphere inside Sidetrack was rather subdued. Joyce and Paul and the rest of the Sidetrack Band were going over their program for the night, and a few people mingled around. It was still early evening, and the sun's rays danced playfully with the shadows. Carissa found no spark for Trevor anywhere. Taking a deep breath, she decided to go someplace completely *different,* someplace kind of upscale.

Making her way down the street, she turned in at Knickerbockers. As she looked around she felt satisfied with her decision. She turned off her cell phone, took a seat at the bar, and ordered a drink.

☆ ☆ ☆

She finally got a call from Trevor at work the next day.

"What were you doing last night?" he asked. "I tried calling you several times, but you had your cell phone off."

Turning her back to the bank's lobby, Carissa lowered her voice and cupped her hand over the phone. "The better question, Trevor, is where were *you* the past several nights? You sure weren't keeping in touch with *me*."

"I tried to call you last night!"

Carissa was a little afraid that Trevor's voice might jump right out of the phone and land in the air around her, where others could hear it. "Listen, I can't talk right now, Trevor. Goodbye!"

Trevor dropped the dead phone and toppled back onto the bed. He'd gotten up early to talk to Carissa, and now he wasn't sure he could go back to sleep. Where had she been? He knew she'd been someplace doing something unimaginable, because she'd turned off her phone. He knew he wasn't making good choices these days, so it stood to reason that she probably wasn't either.

☆ ☆ ☆

Carissa came out of the bathroom, hoping she had covered up her recent bout of tears well enough to face the public. Her phone was ringing when she got back to her desk.

"Carissa! This is Shawn Alt. We met at Knickerbockers last night."

"Oh, yes. Hi, Shawn." Carissa tried to sound bright.

"Hey, I was feeling like having a little fun with somebody beautiful this Friday night, and I thought of you first. Would it be all right if I came by and picked you up around 8:00?"

"Sure! That sounds really fun." Carissa said it almost without thinking.

"Great! I'll see you at 8:00 then."

Shawn had sounded genuinely happy to be talking to her. That was kind of nice, but she felt a tiny bit bad. He wasn't just some guy she'd met—he was one of Trevor's former teammates from Nebraska. She knew it was a little cruel to do this to Trevor, but after all the crying she'd been doing lately she felt as though she deserved to spend a little time with somebody happy.

☆ ☆ ☆

From his vantage point on the mound in the bottom of the ninth inning Trevor spotted a honey-haired girl lingering by the fence. She was watching him, too. In this final game in the BlueClaws series against the Savannah Sand Gnats he was about to wrap up a win. The BlueClaws had just rallied to get three runs and were leading, 8 to 5. Trevor hadn't thrown very many strikes, but the fielders had his back, and he was expecting another win for his record.

José Morban came to the plate for the Sand Gnats. Rob signaled a four-seam fastball, and Trevor sent the pitch in hard and fast over the plate for a strike.

Trevor saw the girl by the fence smile.

His next pitch was a curveball. Morban sliced the air and the ball landed with a gratifying smack in Rob's glove.

Trevor looked over at the girl by the fence one last time. There was something about her; something kind of wholesome. He really wanted to meet her. Using her as motivation to end the game, Trevor delivered his final pitch, a changeup. Again Morban's bat was denied, and the game was over.

Moving off the mound, Trevor walked over to the girl. She seemed a little embarrassed that he had noticed her, but like most girls she wasn't going to turn away from a chance to meet him.

"Hi! What's your name?" Trevor asked.

"I'm Joelle," she said, giving Trevor a once-over with her eyes.

"Did you enjoy the game, Joelle? I saw you watching."

"I love baseball," she confessed, "but I didn't mean to be so obvious that I was watching you. You didn't have to come over here and talk to me."

"But I did!" Trevor quickly replied. "I *did* have to come over and talk to you. You just seemed like a really great girl. Would you like to go get something to eat with me?"

"I'd like that a lot! I'll wait for you outside the gate."

☆ ☆ ☆

It was Monday morning at the bank, and her phone was ringing when she walked in.

It was Trevor. "Carissa, we need to talk."

"Why do you keep calling me at work?"

"I can't reach you any other place. You had your cell phone off again." He paused. "Look, Carissa, I'm really sorry, but I just don't know what's happening right now. I wanted to stop drinking so much, but I've been right back at it lately, and last night I kissed someone."

Trevor hadn't delivered the news with his usual arrogance, but neither had he delivered it with sensitivity. His statement was more a monotone indifference, as though he was resigned to something.

"Well, Trevor, I cheated on you, too," Carissa admitted.

Suddenly he was angry. No monotone. No indifference. *Mad!* "We're through!" he declared, and hung up the phone.

☆ ☆ ☆

The final weeks of the BlueClaws 2001 season were rocky for Trevor and Carissa. They broke up, had clipped conversations, hurled accusations, still thought of each other constantly, dated other people— and got back together right before Trevor returned home the first week of September.

He had ended the season with a 1.13 earned-run average, and had earned a position on the South Atlantic League All-Star team. In 48 games pitching for the BlueClaws he had given up only nine earned runs in 72 innings. In spite of his stellar performance, the BlueClaws finished the season with 60 wins and 72 losses. The Lexington Legends went on to grab the 2001 South Atlantic League Championship title. They won the first two games of a five-game series against the Asheville Tourists before the series was canceled in the wake of the terrorist attacks on September 11.

"Can you believe this?" Trevor said out loud as he watched the television footage of the airplanes flying into the World Trade Center

141

towers. The cameras focused on a tearful girl begging to find out if anybody had knowledge of her boyfriend.

Almost without thinking, Trevor moved to the phone and dialed the number. "Carissa, can you come over? I want to see you. I'm glad we're back together. I love you."

"I love you too, Trevor. I'm glad you're home safe. I want to see you, too."

☆ ☆ ☆

After having such a fantastic minor league season, Trevor was a Lincoln celebrity. Baseball lovers had followed his progress. He didn't know half the people who recognized him when he walked down the street.

One day a guy in a Cornhuskers T-shirt and baseball hat approached him. "Hey, you're Trevor Bullock!"

"Hi, how's it goin'?" Trevor answered, trying to place the guy.

Seeing the blank look on Trevor's face, the man laughed. "I'm Danny McCune. You probably don't remember me. I was a freshman your senior year, and they redshirted me, so I was pretty much in the background."

Trevor smiled. "Oh, well, that explains it. How are things going for you now?"

"I'm doing decent. But *you!* Wow!" Danny shook his head. "What a season *you* had with the BlueClaws!"

Trevor was about to utter his generic thank-you when he saw a faraway look come over Danny's face. "Of course that kind of baseball success comes at a price, doesn't it?"

"A price? I'm not sure I know what you mean." Trevor was a bit confused. Sure, baseball success came at a price, but what self-respecting baseball player wasn't willing to pay it?

"Well, didn't you used to date that girl Carissa Dunn? She seemed like a really great girl. I'm not sure I could stand watching her date guys like Shawn Alt. But I guess that's the sacrifice you make. I guess you can't let anything get in the way of reaching the major league dream."

"No. No, you can't." Trevor managed to say. "Well, it was nice seeing you, Danny."

Turning quickly, he walked in the opposite direction, with no destination in mind. Shawn Alt! Why did this Danny guy think Carissa was dating Shawn Alt? A million thoughts jumped into his mind at once. He contemplated storming into her college class and pulling her out. The thought to call Nate even crossed his mind.

Back in junior high Nate used to always round up a bunch of rough-looking guys to help defend Trevor's honor. Back then Trevor was the one who had messed with somebody else's girlfriend and sometimes needed help in defending himself. Now he was ready to beat Shawn's face in. Would Nate help him again, or was that just too junior high to consider?

Trevor climbed into his Jeep and stormed down the street. He'd think of something! Carissa was *definitely* going to have to answer for this!

☆ ☆ ☆

Carissa answered the door to find Kendra, from her Bible study group, standing there.

"Hey, Kendra, come in!" she said, opening the door wider.

"Shannon tells me that you decided to be baptized while we were at the women's retreat in Grand Island," Kendra said. "I just wanted to stop by and tell you how happy I am to hear that."

"Well, I'm happy about it too," Carissa smiled. "I want to live a new life, Kendra. I've sorta had one foot inside the church and one foot outside for a long time, and I want to change that. The women's retreat really helped me appreciate my Christian friends and see that giving my life to Christ is the only way to live."

"How do you feel about Saturday being the Sabbath?" Kendra had asked the big question.

"Well, I've thought about that a lot," Carissa admitted. "Sometimes I've tried to tell myself that it doesn't matter what day I worship God as long as I pick one out of the seven."

"You mean, it could be Wednesday or Sunday or whichever day

you wanted, as long as you celebrated Sabbath at least one time during the week?"

Carissa nodded. "I tried to tell myself that for a while, but then I realized that God had picked the day of the week so I wouldn't have to. I'm not very good at sticking with right choices. I know that if it were left up to me I'd promise to give God Sunday, but then something would come up, and I'd promise Him Monday, only to forget. Does that make any sense? I think God did me a favor when He picked the day of the week for me, because now I can't make excuses. It's very clear."

Kendra nodded. "I like the way you've thought about it."

"It's as though God has made a date with me," Carissa added. "He loves me and wants to spend time with me so much that He set aside the time and asks me to do the same."

"Speaking of dates, what's the status with Trevor?"

"Well, I'm dating him still—or again. Whichever."

"Carissa, how does he make you feel, really?"

"I love him so much, but as I grow closer to you and the others at church I don't know." She sighed, then finished her thought. "I wish Trevor and I had a really common desire to change our lives. Sometimes I've thought he did want to change, but, well, I know this sounds mean, but he's still so selfish."

"Carissa, nobody can make a relationship work with a fundamentally selfish person. I mean, we're all fundamentally selfish, but you deserve a relationship with somebody who, by God's grace, wants to overcome his selfishness. You deserve to be loved!"

"You're right," Carissa agreed. "But I keep thinking Trevor might be heading in the right direction, and I keep hoping that if I wait a little longer he'll come around."

Kendra gave Carissa a rueful smile and left.

A few minutes later a knock sounded at the door. Actually, it wasn't so much a knock as a pounding demand for immediate attention. When Carissa opened the door—there stood Trevor.

"Hi," she said weakly. The look in his eyes made any other words catch in her throat.

"Tell me about Shawn Alt. *Now!*"

Her head began to spin. How had he found out? Realizing that her stunned silence was not at all reassuring, she said, "Come in, please. I don't want to have this conversation out here for the whole world to hear . . . Listen, I dated Shawn for about three weeks."

"What were you doing dating him for even three *minutes*?" Trevor shouted.

"I told you I cheated on you, Trevor," Carissa said calmly. "But for most of those three weeks you and I were broken up!"

"We break up, and you immediately find one of my former teammates to pass the time with? Do I mean so little to you that you would find somebody new the next *day*? And Shawn Alt! What a loser! He's a terrible baseball player, and he's ugly! What were you thinking, Carissa?"

"Like I said, I saw him for only three weeks. A lot of the other ballplayers really bit my head off about it, and it didn't take long for me to discover that I didn't want to continue seeing him; it only made me want to get back together with you, Trevor. It only made me miss *you* more."

Trevor was silent.

"I haven't gone to a bar or had a drink since I ended things with Shawn. Dating him only made me want to study my Bible more and give God my life for good. I'm making plans to be baptized." She picked up her Bible. "Listen to this, Trevor. It's Psalm 103:12: *'As far as the east is from the west, so far has he removed our transgressions from us.'* I want to be a different person. I want to be separated from my transgressions. I'm sorry you found out about this, but I'm not sorry it happened, because it made me finally surrender my life to Jesus."

"But why didn't you tell me about Shawn yourself?" Trevor asked. He had calmed down, but he wasn't ready to let go of his anger completely. Besides, it felt strange hearing Carissa talk like this about Jesus.

"I didn't tell you, Trevor, because I didn't want to hurt you. I didn't tell you because I didn't think you needed to know. I wanted to forget it ever happened."

"Yeah, well, I found out from a perfect stranger!" Trevor retorted. "That was *sooo* much better, Carissa!"

"I'm sorry, Trevor. I didn't mean to hurt you." Carissa was crying.

Trevor looked at her. Who was this person? When he left for the

2001 season she'd been drinking like a sailor on leave. Now she was talking about being baptized and surrendering her life. Suddenly he knew why this made him so uncomfortable. He'd never say it out loud, but he was a little threatened by the fact that Carissa seemed to be more committed to Christ than he was. For a moment his conscience reminded him that he'd cheated on Carissa on a regular basis. And he still went to bars. He still liked to party. He wasn't nearly so far along on the path to change as Carissa was. For the first time in his life he realized that Carissa deserved a man who would be honest and treat her better. "Carissa, we need to let each other go," he said finally. "I don't think I can get over you dating Shawn, and I'm not sure I'm the right man for you anyway. We need to break up and mean it this time."

Carissa's crying took on a new intensity.

Trevor turned and let himself out of the apartment.

Chapter 16

Thi is is for the best, Carissa," Lisa Shafer said. "I don't want you fretting over Trevor anymore. Cheryl, Kendra, and I know a guy who's coming into town this weekend. His name is Russ Knapton—I want you to meet him. Go out with him; see how it goes. He's a really nice guy."

"OK," Carissa agreed dully.

It had been five days since she and Trevor had broken up. She agreed with Lisa that it was for the best, but she still loved him—she just did. She wondered how he was doing. Telling herself that it wasn't any big deal to check up on him, she dialed his cell phone.

"Hi, Trevor. I was just thinking of you and wanted to call."

"Hey! Thanks!" He sounded genuinely happy to hear from her.

But no sooner had Trevor answered the phone than she doubted her own sanity for placing the call. In the background she could hear the familiar boisterous sound of Cornhusker fans getting revved up for their home game the next day. The sound of the Sidetrack Band launching into "There Is No Place Like Nebraska" was unmistakable.

"Are you at Sidetrack, Trevor?" Carissa fumed.

Trevor jumped off the bar stool and hurried outside. "No, no. Not really. I just peeked in is all. I want to change, Carissa. I'm not going to drink anymore, and I'm not going to party."

"You are so full of it, Trevor!" Carissa shot back. "That's just a bunch of baloney! I can still hear the people around you partying!"

Trevor looked out at the scene on the street and realized that indeed the mood was festive and the air was filled with the raucous joy of the home game. There was no way out of this one.

"You're such a loser, Trevor! Just go! Run off to your bars and drink your life away! I don't care! I'm so sick of this! I can't even believe I called you!" She flipped her phone shut and threw it, *hard*, into the couch cushions.

☆ ☆ ☆

At 1:30 a.m. the phone rang.

"Carissa? I'm *soooo* soooorry." Trevor was terribly drunk. Aaron had brought Trevor with him to his apartment, and Trevor had stepped out into the parking lot to call Carissa. He was devastated by the realization that his relationship might really be over with her this time.

"You're drunk out of your mind! Go to bed!" she said in disgust.

She was about to hang up when he bawled into the phone, "I plan on going to church."

"I don't believe you, Trevor! You're three sheets to the wind right now, and I can't imagine that you're ever going to change. I am so done with this!"

"I'm just going to drive home and die," he said pitifully. "Goodbye, Carissa."

She pulled the pillow over her head. "Why should I still care about this drunk?" Then another thought hit her: What if he got behind the wheel, drunk as he was? "God forbid he dies—or kills somebody else," she muttered. "I'd feel terrible."

She switched on a light and threw on jeans and a sweater. Grabbing her keys, she fumed, "Why do I care?"

Trevor was standing by his Jeep when Carissa drove into the parking lot at Aaron's apartment. She felt her heart flutter. For reasons she could never explain, she loved him. But she determined that she was not going to be her typical emotional self. This had gone on long enough, and she wasn't going to stand for it any longer. She steeled her mind against giving in to more than driving him home. This time she'd be calling the shots.

"What are you doing?" she demanded as she got out of her car.

"I feel aaaawful!" Trevor slurred.

"How much did you drink, anyway?" Carissa asked.

"I don't know . . . Twelve shots of Jäger, maybe."

"Are you serious? . . . No! Actually, you're ridiculous!" Carissa was shaking. Was it from anger? sadness? shock? Who knew? "I am so glad you and I are done! You made the right decision for us!"

"I don't know why I broke up with you."

"Well, I'm glad you did!" Carissa snapped. "You are such a loser, Trevor!"

"Can we try to work things out?" he pleaded.

"No way! There is no way I'm getting into this with you again! Forget it, Trevor! We're through!" She strode back to her car. "Get in. I'm taking you home."

Trevor swayed over to the passenger side and slumped into the seat. He lowered his head into his hands. "How can I live without you?" he wept.

She had *never* seen him be this vulnerable. Fighting off the urge to cry herself, she said firmly, "Trevor, I'm taking you home. You need to dry out."

"Can I talk to you tomorrow?" Trevor pleaded.

"Maybe—I don't know."

"I love you, Carissa."

"Good night, Trevor."

☆ ☆ ☆

"You look exhausted!" Cheryl gave Carissa a hug as she came into the Sabbath school classroom.

"Yeah, I know. I didn't sleep well last night." She wasn't interested in getting into the details. She was just glad to be in church.

"Is everything all right? I know you just broke up with Trevor, but I hate to see you losing sleep over him. Remember, we set you up with Russ Knapton tonight. Several of us are getting together for a game night at Shannon's house. I hope you'll enjoy meeting and getting to know him."

Carissa smiled weakly. "Thank you. I'm looking forward to meeting him."

Ardyce spotted Carissa after church and pulled her into her office. "I'll tell you the truth, Carissa. I don't want Trevor to screw things up with you and lose you, but I don't expect you to wait around for him to pull his head out."

The tears that seemed to always be on the surface these days began to roll down her cheeks.

"I saw you bring him back last night." She gave Carissa a squeeze. "Thank you. He's pretty broken up that you're mad at him, but I'm on your side with this. You don't have to put up with his foolishness." Ardyce spoke with all the blunt moxie of her German heritage. "And I told him, 'You're a fool if you don't see what a special girl Carissa is. But if you're not going to change, she'd be a fool to stick with you.'"

"How's he doing today?"

Ardyce waved her hand in disgust. "Oh, he's sleeping it off. I raised him better than this!"

Carissa almost had to laugh. There wasn't a more fiercely loyal mama out there, yet it seemed that even Ardyce had had it with Trevor.

"I sort of told him I'd talk with him more this afternoon," Carissa admitted. "But some of the other girls have asked me to meet another guy tonight. I said I would, so I plan on keeping my word."

"You go right ahead." Ardyce hugged her again. "I hope you have a good time."

When Carissa drove up to the Bullocks' house later that afternoon, Trevor stepped out of the house and slid into her car. "Can we just go for a drive?"

"Sure." She wasn't sure what to expect from this conversation. Before coming, though, she had decided again to deal with Trevor at arm's length.

"My mom's kind of mad at me," he began.

"Yes. She told me."

Trevor stared out the window. It was impossible to determine what he was thinking. For years he'd been hiding his emotions on the mound, and now it was as if he had no idea how to stop hiding. She doubted that he'd ever stop putting on the game face, and she wasn't sure she could deal with somebody who was that self-enclosed.

"I really do want to change," he said finally. "I want to come to church with you. It's a little hard for me to see you getting all connected with the young adults there while I'm still an outsider in my own church. I don't know how well I'll do making friends at church, but I want to try."

"Why *would* people at church like you, Trevor?" Carissa's voice was hard. "You're so full of yourself and strut around like you think you're the man and everybody ought to bow at your feet. You think that because you play baseball everybody should be so impressed, and all the while you're going out on Friday nights, partying, and knocking back 12 shots of Jägermeister!"

Her voice broke, but she continued doggedly. "You don't have anything in common with the people in church, and you don't *act* as if church people and their ideas are important to you."

He nodded dully and continued to stare out the window. Fall colors lingered on the trees, and the deep shadows of late afternoon were beginning to gather. "I think I'd like to change that. I think I'd like to try to find something in common with your friends at church. Most of all, I want to have things in common with you. Please, Carissa, can we try to make this work?"

"If I take you back, there has got to be a testing period," Carissa replied firmly. "I know it sounds blunt, but you'll be on probation."

"OK. I can accept that." Trevor's voice had a strange kind of quiet to it.

"Another thing. My friends at church have invited me to meet a guy from out of state tonight, and I want to keep my promise to go out with them and meet him."

"That's fine," Trevor said meekly. "Thank you for taking this drive with me."

☆ ☆ ☆

The mood was light when Carissa arrived. The family room buzzed with friendly conversation, and the smell of popcorn filled the air.

"Hi, Carissa!" Lisa greeted. "Russ is here somewhere." She looked toward the kitchen and called, "Russ, come here!"

A broadly built guy shifted out of the kitchen and approached.

"This is Carissa Dunn," Lisa smiled. "Carissa, this is Russ Knapton."

"Hi," Carissa said. Russ seemed pleasant, but he wasn't nearly as good-looking as Trevor. She brushed the thought aside. Why should she care if a guy was as good-looking as Trevor? That wasn't the point.

"C'mon," Russ invited. "Let's join the others who are playing Pictionary. I hope you are really smart, because I'm not the greatest at drawing."

Carissa laughed. "We'll give it a try."

Throughout the evening they kept up an easy dialogue. Russ seemed interested in Carissa, in who she was and what she hoped for in life. He shared what God had done in his life and encouraged her to keep turning to Christ during the difficult times. He looked her in the eye when he talked, making her feel as though he valued her and wanted to hear what she had to say. It was incredibly refreshing being with him. It made her sad to realize that Trevor had never treated her with the kind of respect this stranger was showing her.

☆ ☆ ☆

It was well past midnight, and Trevor's light was still on. Ardyce peeked through the slightly ajar door and choked back tears—Trevor was reading his Bible.

"Love is patient, love is kind. It does not envy, it does not boast, it is not proud. It is not rude, it is not self-seeking, it is not easily angered, it keeps no record of wrongs. Love does not delight in evil but rejoices with the truth. It always protects, always trusts, always hopes, always perseveres" (1 Corinthians 13:4-7).

He closed the Book. The idea distilled slowly in his mind that he had perhaps never loved anybody . . . never not been proud or self-seeking . . . always been more than willing to get angry and keep a record of wrongs. Especially with Carissa. He wasn't positive that he could actually turn around on a dime and begin behaving and thinking in a loving manner, but he wanted to. For the first time he wanted to head in a loving direction.

Grabbing his keys, he left the house and got into his Jeep.

☆ ☆ ☆

152

Carissa couldn't stop thinking about everything that made Russ different from anyone she had ever been with before. She hadn't really been drawn to him, but he had started her thinking. Was it possible to find a nice guy like Russ who also gave her a feeling of passion? Or was it better to sacrifice passion for truly being treated well?

A knock sounded at her door. She ran her fingers through her hair and squinted through the peephole. Trevor stood on the welcome mat, holding a dozen red roses.

"I got these for you," he said when she opened the door. "I'm sorry, Carissa. I'm sorry I've hurt you. I'm sorry that although I've claimed to love you a million times, I've never really treated you with love. I'm not going to promise you that I won't mess up a million more times, but I want to love you better. I'm sorry I've been so self-centered."

☆ ☆ ☆

"Mr. Bullock, will you sign my jersey?" A young boy approached Trevor at the University of Nebraska pitching camp, toting a Cornhuskers "Bullock" jersey.

"Sure." Trevor smiled and took the jersey.

"Are you going to play in the majors?" the boy asked, an eager grin lighting his face.

"Yes, I am!" Trevor replied, playfully flipping the bill of the boy's cap. "I'll be the one they call on to shut down Barry Bonds in the bottom of the ninth inning!"

"Thanks, Mr. Bullock!" the boy called over his shoulder as he ran to show his parents the signed jersey.

"Those kids remind me of myself." Scott Fries, a former Cornhusker teammate, had been watching the exchange between Trevor and the young fan. "I love coming to these camps during the off-season and helping these kids. I'm glad Coach Childress invites us every year."

"Yeah, it feels good," Trevor agreed.

"So where do you think you'll go after spring training this year?"

"I think they'll send me to either the high-A Clearwater Threshers or AA Reading Phillies. I had a pretty good year at Lakewood."

"Well, I hope it all works out for you." Scott pointed out toward the field. "Look at those kids!"

Following the sweep of Scott's arm, Trevor saw two boys pitching left-handed. One wore a "Fries" jersey, and the other sported a jersey that read "Bullock" as clear as day:

☆ ☆ ☆

"Mom, I'm reading this Daniel 7, 8, and 9 stuff, and I have to admit that it's a little hard to follow." Trevor frowned over his open Bible. "I know it's a big deal to the Adventist Church, but I'm just not sure I get it."

"Well, keep studying," Ardyce encouraged. "You have to always keep studying your Bible and searching for truth. I wouldn't want you to just take somebody else's interpretation and make it your own. You'll find your own way."

Giving Trevor a proud-mama smile, Ardyce added, "I can't even believe you're diving into a subject like the 2300-day prophecy. That's some pretty meaty stuff."

"Well, if I'm going to claim to be a Seventh-day Adventist, then I need to know whether I really agree with what the church teaches. I'm not going to believe *some* of the Adventist doctrines; I need to believe them all. And I've got to find the answers in the Bible. I've got to know *why* I believe something."

Ardyce wanted to ask him what he thought of playing baseball on Sabbath, but she didn't. It was clear that her son was under conviction by the Holy Spirit, and she knew that God would convict him about the Sabbath when the time was right. So instead she said, "I feel like I'm finally talking with an adult. I'm so happy to see you studying and forming your own beliefs."

A few weeks later Carissa was baptized by Pastor Shannon Minnick in the College View Seventh-day Adventist Church in Lincoln. Her friends still weren't too sure about Trevor—and he was rather reserved around them—but they all stood together in support of her decision.

Ardyce was thrilled. She gave Carissa a New International Version Women of Faith Bible for a remembrance of this special day.

Chapter 17

want to get dessert," Carissa said with a sparkle in her eyes.

"OK," Trevor agreed.

They had come to Grandma's House on Lowell Street in Lincoln to enjoy a dinner together. Carissa felt some of the day's stress melt into a feeling of comfort in the warm atmosphere of the restaurant. After ordering her dessert, she sat back. "How's your arm doing? When you were playing all the time, you used to complain that it hurt a lot."

"It feels OK," Trevor said. "I try not to push it too hard. But I don't want to get out of shape either, so sometimes it still hurts."

"Still throwing a lot of pitches with your dad?"

"Oh, yeah! He's not going to let me slow down. No rust allowed on these joints." He grinned, flexing his elbow.

The waiter set Carissa's dessert in front of her. She picked up her spoon in anticipation of the sweet pleasure awaiting her. When she looked down, sitting in the middle of the neatly decorated dish was an engagement ring.

Trevor slipped down on one knee. "Will you marry me, Carissa?"

A surge of excitement pulsed through Carissa as she realized what was happening. With a happy cry she exclaimed, "Yes!" and threw her arms around his neck in a happy embrace.

As she lay in bed later that night she thought, *What am I going to say to my mom?* Here she was engaged, and she wasn't even sure she wanted to tell anybody. Her mother had been there for her through all the tears. She had seen Trevor destroying her daughter's joy, so there was no way she was going to be happy about this. And what about her church friends? What would they say? True, she'd seen a lot of growth in Trevor recently, but she'd also seen him leave for six months to play baseball. It seemed that he no sooner set foot back into that world than his commitment to Christ crumbled—to say nothing of his commitment to *her*.

Toying with the ring on her finger, Carissa felt a heavy dread fill her mind and land with a thud in her stomach. She didn't want to doubt Trevor, but all those months ago he'd left her with a "promise" ring, and look how well *that* promise had been kept! Maybe he was hoping *this* ring would keep her out of trouble while he was gone—gone, and not wearing a ring himself. She was all too aware that Trevor was leaving again in three months.

"You asked her to *marry* you?" Nate was incredulous. "Whaddya do that for?"

"Carissa is really important to me," Trevor insisted.

"Important, yes. But everybody knows that baseball is your top priority, Trevor. And excuse me, dude, but I just can't see you tying yourself down."

"Well, maybe I'm changing."

"No, you're not!" Nate laughed. "You aren't capable of dating only one girl."

"I love her, Nate," Trevor said.

"OK, all right; you love her. Fine. But let me tell you, I think getting married is the stupidest thing anybody can do. Look at my folks—they were married for 30 years and then got divorced. I mean, what's the point? You don't need some piece of paper to tell you you're in love. You've done a lot of stupid things in your life, Trevor, but this has got to be the dumbest one yet. All you're going to do is end up breaking her heart when you cheat on her, and then you're going to have alimony to pay on top of it."

"Well, thank you for your thoughts, Nate!" Trevor said hotly. "You can choose not to get married if you want to, but I want to get married someday. And I want to marry Carissa."

156

"I'm so *happy!*" Ardyce enveloped Carissa in a hearty hug.

Well, at least someone is happy, Carissa thought. She had halfheartedly reported the news to her friends in the Sabbath school class, and they had halfheartedly congratulated her. Trevor had to have noticed the lack of enthusiasm. She wished so much that he could fit in better at church, but so far he still seemed rather withdrawn. Well, who could blame him; he was going to be gone for half the year, so why put down roots?

Carissa smiled at Ardyce. "Thanks for caring for me."

"I *do* care for you!" Ardyce said warmly. "But I really think you and Trevor can make something special together if you stay close to the Lord. I'm truly happy for both of you."

When Trevor broke the news of his engagement to his dad, Duaine looked up blankly and said, "Why?"

"Well—" Trevor searched for the right words.

His dad waved him off. "You had a fantastic season with Lakewood. Let's just focus on getting your pitching to the next level. C'mon, let's go practice outside."

☆ ☆ ☆

"*In his hand is the life of every creature and the breath of all mankind. . . . To God belong wisdom and power; counsel and understanding are his. What he tears down cannot be rebuilt; the man he imprisons cannot be released. . . . He leads counselors away stripped and makes fools of judges. . . . He leads priests away stripped and overthrows men long established. He silences the lips of trusted advisers and takes away the discernment of elders. He pours contempt on nobles and disarms the mighty. He reveals the deep things of darkness and brings deep shadows into the light. . . . He deprives the leaders of the earth of their reason; he sends them wandering through a trackless waste*" (Job 12:10-24).

Trevor set his Bible down and stared out the window for a long time. His half-packed bags lay open on the bed. He would leave for Clearwater, Florida, in a couple days for spring training.

This morning he had felt drawn to Job 12. It wasn't Job's suffering that drew him; it was the way God's character was revealed in the book. Chapter 12 seemed to be speaking especially to him. All this business about God being in control of everything, and no matter how high one climbs on the ladder of human prestige God can bring you down with just a thought if He so chooses . . . It was a radical idea for Trevor, but it made sense. It's far better to live for God and be a part of the kingdom of heaven than to seek worldly greatness.

The passage reminded him of a verse Rob Avila had shown him:

"This is what the Lord says: 'Let not the wise man boast of his wisdom or the strong man boast of his strength or the rich man boast of his riches, but let him who boasts boast about this: that he understands and knows me, that I am the Lord, who exercises kindness, justice and righteousness on earth, for in these I delight,' declares the Lord" (Jeremiah 9:23, 24).

He began to pray. More than anything else, he wanted to boast about knowing and understanding God.

When Carissa answered a knock on her door later, there was Trevor, a strange look on his face. What was it? Peaceful? Determined? Empowered? Frightened?

"Can I come in?"

"Yes. Of course. What's up?"

Trevor slumped onto the couch. Sitting down beside him, Carissa asked again, "What's up? You look—I don't know . . . You look like something's up."

"Carissa, I wanted to tell you first." Trevor took her hand and just held it. Drawing in a deep breath, he looked into her face. "I'm not going back to Clearwater. I want to stay right here in Lincoln with you. I've decided to give up playing professional baseball."

Her lips began to quiver. She wasn't sure she had heard correctly. "What—what are you saying?"

"I said I'm quitting baseball."

Joy and disbelief—and disappointment—raced across her face. "But baseball is your whole life! Trevor, why? Why are you quitting? Where is this coming from? Do you mean it?"

"Yes, Carissa, I mean it," he said firmly. "I've actually been think-ing about it for a long time. I kept working out and throwing pitches with my dad so I could contemplate this in peace. I wanted to decide on my own, and I didn't want to hear everyone's comments on the subject until I had decided for myself. It may seem as if this is coming out of nowhere, but I've been thinking about it for a long time."

He picked up her Bible from the end table. As he thumbed through it, he said, "All winter I've kept coming back to this verse in Hebrews: '*If we deliberately keep on sinning after we have received the knowledge of the truth, no sacrifice for sins is left*'" (10:26).

"The Lord has really been sanctifying and working on my heart," Trevor confessed. "I want to make a conscious effort to spend time with Him, and I think that's what the Sabbath is all about—time with God. I don't want to keep spending Sabbath time on other things, on baseball and parties. I don't want to keep sinning now that I know the truth."

"I love you, Trevor," Carissa whispered.

"I love you, too, Carissa—too much to leave again. I know that if I left I'd be faced with the same temptations I faced before. I know I'd skip church, play ball on the Sabbath, get drunk, hook up with easy women—it sounds pathetic, but I can't control myself when I'm out there in the limelight. I love all the attention. I love feeling like I control the game. But the longer I'm out there the more I fall in love with myself and out of love with God. And that just scares me. I've got to leave that life and begin a new life, beginning now."

Carissa buried her face in Trevor's chest and wept. The one thing she never would have asked of him he was choosing on his own. The words she wanted most to hear from him he was saying. For the first time in her life she was hearing Trevor say that his love for God and his love for her were more important than baseball. It was unthinkable, but it was happening.

That evening Trevor found his mom in the family room. He said nothing for a moment; then the words came out in a rush. "I'm not leaving in a couple days after all, Mom. . . . I'm not going back to play baseball, because I don't want to lose what I've just started with God. I don't want to turn away from the Holy Spirit when He speaks to my heart. And I don't want to lose Carissa. I've sat on the fence for a long time, hoping I could have it all in both worlds, but I can't, and I've got to get off the fence."

Ardyce sat in stunned silence as a flood of thoughts poured into her head all at once. "Are—are you sure you can do this?" she stammered. "I mean, are you positive you won't regret it?"

"I've asked God to take away my desire for baseball, for that competitive edge I always feel, but to let me keep loving the game," Trevor said quietly. "I think He's done that for me. I know I wouldn't be able to walk away from baseball if I thought I was going to regret it. I think it will be fine, Mom. I know this is what I want to do."

Ardyce leaned over and pulled Trevor into one of her tight hugs. "You've made the right choice, son," she affirmed. "Walking with Christ and sharing your life's journey with a godly wife are the two most important things you can do, far more important than fame and fortune. I know this had to be a very hard decision for you to make, but it's the right one."

She released him and sat back. "I've prayed for you every day, and I know God has never left your side. He never will."

Trevor broke the news to his dad over dinner at Chili's. Duaine Bullock looked at his son as though he had suddenly become a stranger. Then his eyes dropped to his food. Why did Trevor have to ruin a perfectly good meal with such perfectly outrageous news? Did he somehow think that mixing devastating news with food might make it easier to swallow? Certainly he couldn't actually mean that he was giving up baseball for *good!*

"If you take a break this year, you won't be able to get back in," Duaine said ominously. "Don't be foolish, Trevor. You're already older than a lot of the guys on the team."

"I'm not hoping to get back in," Trevor said deliberately. "I'm not planning to play professional baseball ever again."

"You've spent your whole *life* planning to play professional baseball!" Duaine's voice rose angrily before he pulled it back down into the controlled range. "You can't quit now. You've gotta see how far you can go with this. You had a great season last year, and I know you're mad they didn't invite you to the Arizona fall league, but you haven't peaked yet. You're only getting better."

Trevor shook his head. "Dad, I'm not going back. I know I could make the majors if I went back, but that's just not what's important to me anymore."

"You're going to let that church and a *woman* steal your dream?" Duaine was becoming too furious to even really speak. Worst of all, Trevor's decision was allowing the Seventh-day Adventist Church and Carissa to steal his dream. Hadn't he spent countless hours tossing balls with Trevor, grooming him, cheering for him at every single high school and college game, with the exception of maybe one or two? He'd already planned his trips so that he could watch Trevor in the coming season. He'd sent him to pitching camps and saved four boxfuls of newspaper clippings and other baseball memorabilia over the years. His son had a natural gift—something you couldn't teach, something you had to just believe in and be thankful for. He had beautiful control. If Duaine believed anything about God, it was that He had made his son special, had given him a special gift and placed him on the earth to play baseball and blessed him with that magical left arm. Didn't Christians claim that it brought glory to God to use their gifts? Had God ever shown any sign of being upset that Trevor pitched on Saturday? Did Trevor have a higher ERA on Saturdays? Duaine didn't think so.

Why hadn't Trevor at least *discussed* this with him? This business of dropping a bomb over dinner made him feel as if his point of view didn't matter, as if *he* didn't matter. Anything could have happened, Duaine realized. Trevor could have been injured, or the team could have decided to dump him. But you don't just *quit.* You let someone else tell you you're finished. You reach for the prize until the prize disappears. You don't just walk away from it.

"You'll have to give back that Jeep Cherokee," Duaine said. He stood up and strode from the table, his mind reeling. His thoughts could find no place to land and take root as they exploded in his head. He just wished Trevor would have *discussed* it with him. . . .

In some sort of senseless homicidal act, it seemed that the Adventist Church had taken his son from him . . . stolen his joy . . . destroyed his dream. The church already owned his wife. How much more of himself was he going to have to sacrifice on the altar of this greedy religion that stole a man's life? It would be a very long time—if ever—before he would darken the door of an Adventist Church again. Enough was enough!

161

Later that evening Duaine sat sullenly in the family room. Ardyce caught and held her husband's eye. She knew he would take the news hard. Even so, it was somehow shocking to see the cold stone wall that was now Duaine's face. At one level she was angry that Trevor's own father—her husband—couldn't see past his own disappointment long enough to support his son in whatever choice he made. Certainly she had stood by Trevor with love when he was making choices that disappointed her.

Duaine caught her look. "Look, Ardyce, I just don't get it. All his life he wants to play baseball, starting with T-ball. He gets the opportunities—and then he makes the decision he does, and he quits playing!"

"It's not fair what you're doing, Duaine!" Ardyce said. "You're trying to live your own dreams through your son."

"No, I'm not!"

She continued without a pause. "You want to see him make millions of dollars and be famous, even if it kills his soul in the process."

The color drained from Duaine's face. "I don't know what you are talking about!" he thundered. "I just see the talent he has and don't want to see it thrown away! What a waste!"

Chapter 18

Rod Nichols here, Trevor. Listen, I hear you've decided to leave the organization. Is there something we can do? I'd like for you to come back."

Trevor adjusted the phone at his ear. "No, Coach; you heard right. I'm quitting pro ball."

"Well, now, explain this to me, will you?"

Trevor took a deep breath. "I'm a Seventh-day Adventist, Coach," he said. "For a long time I pretended that being true to my convictions didn't really matter, but I discovered during this past off-season that I really don't want to compromise my convictions any longer. It's important to me to keep my Sabbath holy, from sundown Friday to sundown Saturday. And I can't very well keep the Sabbath holy and play minor league ball."

"Ah, well, is that all?" the coach said heartily. "C'mon, Bullock, we can work with that. You're a relief pitcher. We don't have to put you in on Friday nights or Saturdays." Coach Nichols sounded pleased that the thing could be resolved so easily.

"Yeah, but what happens when the score is tied, 2-2, on a Friday night in a key game? Can you promise me salvation?"

No; he could not.

In call after call Trevor had to explain himself again and again.

"Mr. Bullock! Hello! My name is Stewart Adams. I'm calling from the Chicago Cubs organization. We'd like to talk with you about signing on with us . . ."

"Well, hi there. This is Steve Jones, calling from the Atlanta Braves."

Offers were made. Hefty signing bonuses were mentioned. Reminders were dropped of others Trevor knew who now played in the big leagues for $225,000 to $550,000 their first year up. "I didn't know salvation came with a price," he replied more firmly each time. "You're asking me to give up beliefs for the sake of baseball. I know what I'm giving up, and I know what I'm keeping."

Duaine slumped down at the table. The sunlight streaming through the kitchen window reflected off a new covering of late February snow, but there was nothing bright about Duaine's demeanor.

"Ardyce," he asked casually, "Trevor must have a new cell phone number. What is it?"

"You want to call Trevor?" Ardyce smiled with relief. "That's good, Duaine, really good. You're killing him with your silence. He cares so much about you, you know. Thank you for opening your heart to him again. I know he'll be so glad to hear from you."

He took the number she jotted down with a mumbled "Thanks" and headed for the basement, where he picked up the phone. "Thanks for waiting, Mr. Jackson. Here's Trevor's new number. Maybe you can talk some sense into him. Where did you say you were calling from? . . . The Minnesota Twins? . . . Well, good, good . . . Give Trevor a call."

All day long Duaine gave out Trevor's new number to scouts and prospects who called the house in search of Trevor. Maybe one of them would get through to his son. As for himself, he had no desire to speak to Trevor.

"What are you talking about? What are you doing? You're about to get set for life and you're *quitting?*" Nate was totally blindsided.

Trevor had stopped by to pick him up in the Jeep. Duaine hadn't bothered to come for it, so Trevor decided to keep driving it. He hoped that the confines of a car would keep his feisty cousin a little more in check with his reaction.

"Nate, I just couldn't keep living that life. Things change, you know? I hated what I was becoming. I care too much about my relationship with God and Carissa to let minor league baseball destroy it. These past six months, studying my Bible and reaching out to God and working things out with Carissa, have been the happiest six months of my life!"

Nate could hear the sincerity in Trevor's voice. "Dude, I understand. You gotta see, though, that I was just waiting for the tickets." He grinned, then turned sober again. "I could just see it—you on the mound, and your dad and Aaron and me sitting in the stands for your major league debut. It was just a matter of time."

Trevor's mouth curved slightly into a wistful smile. Nate would have to let the vision go.

But Nate wasn't quite ready to. He gave a little laugh. "I wanted to see you on ESPN, standing there on the mound all cocky and full of yourself. I wanted to see you pitch the ball and have the batter hit a long bomb off you. And then I'd call you and tease you for looking like a fool on national television!" Turning to look full at Trevor, he said quietly, "This is your life, man. You gotta do what you gotta do. If this choice makes you happy, then I'm glad you did it. I mean, you gotta make yourself happy. I guess if you felt that guilty every night, going out after games, I guess you had to make this decision. But I still can't believe it. I never saw this coming."

☆ ☆ ☆

Aaron shook his head, trying to grasp what Trevor had just told him. It wasn't exactly a complete surprise—Trevor had called him several times from Lakewood to share how tired and empty he felt and to talk about how much his arm was hurting. It probably had been just a matter of time before he had had to make this difficult decision. Even so, it still felt as though it had come out of left field.

He pulled on his jacket and decided to take a walk. Maybe the cool air would help him clear his head. He could understand that Trevor wanted a simpler life—that he *needed* to take it back a step or two for his own mental health. He was going to have to do something dramatically different if he was to find the happiness he was seeking. Now that he thought about it, Aaron knew Trevor had been feeling as if a big part of his life were missing when he had been in Lakewood. He knew Trevor wanted to evaluate how important the various things were: baseball, Carissa, God. Now Trevor was evidently thinking in terms of what was really going to bring him the most joy for the rest of his life, and Aaron didn't doubt that he was getting his priorities in the correct order and had made the right choice.

Aaron also knew that he wasn't going to be able to make peace with Trevor's choice overnight. Did Trevor even realize how many people's dreams he'd burned? Did he even care? Take Nate, for example. Nate was a great ballplayer, but an injury in college had knocked him back. As for himself, Aaron had run out of college eligibility and lost his own chance at moving up through the system. And what about Trevor's dad? Had there been anything else he had ever dreamed about for his son? Certainly not!

What Trevor had chosen was sucking up the light of hope for a lot of people. A lot of people had lost the dream in their own life when their wagon had come unhitched from Trevor Bullock's star. And now their star had been sucked into a black hole, never to shine again.

☆ ☆ ☆

What am I going to do now? The question had dangled unanswered in Trevor's mind for days. It would be nice if God would honor his decision with some glorious answer, some amazing job, say, that paid hundreds of thousands of dollars a year, or a massive inheritance from a great-aunt he hadn't known he'd had. Wouldn't it be great to be able to march up to his dad and say, "See? Look how God blesses those who stand for Him!" But so far God had remained unnervingly silent on the subject of blessing Trevor with a great financial windfall. Instead, he found himself doing valet parking at a parking garage and finishing up his criminal justice degree at the University of Nebraska. Without baseball he had no identity, and he was struggling to form a new image of himself.

Even so, God wasn't completely silent in his life. He was speaking to Trevor daily in different ways, comforting him, guiding him, blessing him with Carissa's love and the steadfast devotion of his mother. He searched his Bible daily and was discovering that all God's promises are true. His friend Chad Sadowski had once reminded him that God was always by his side saying, "You'll be all right; I'll take care of you." Now he took comfort in knowing that Chad had been absolutely right about God.

He discovered words of affirmation and comfort everywhere in the Bible:

"My soul finds rest in God alone; my salvation comes from him. He alone is my rock and my salvation; he is my fortress, I will never be shaken" (Psalm 62:1, 2).

" 'For I know the plans I have for you,' declares the Lord, 'plans to prosper you and not to harm you, plans to give you hope and a future' " (Jeremiah 29:11).

"Look at the birds of the air; they do not sow or reap or store away in barns, and yet your heavenly Father feeds them. Are you not much more valuable than they?" (Matthew 6:26).

"I can do everything through him who gives me strength" (Philippians 4:13).

For sure, it wasn't going to be a smooth road, but Trevor never looked back after leaving baseball. He shared his decision with kids at various Adventist gatherings and formed new friendships at church. He turned his gaze toward a future with God as his number one passion and purpose. All the competitive energy he had poured into baseball became an ever-growing love for the God who had saved him from himself.

On December 22, 2002, Trevor and Carissa were married, with Aaron serving as Trevor's best man. Ardyce looked at the happy couple with joy-filled eyes. And Duaine? Well, he made the best of it. He even gave Carissa a hug.

☆ ☆ ☆

"Oooooooh!" Carissa moaned as she hit the snooze button. "I don't want to go to work."

She and Trevor had just returned to their tiny one-bedroom apartment after honeymooning at the Moon Palace Resort in Cancun, Mexico. Reality was fast setting in. She didn't feel like going back to work—and Trevor didn't have a job. Nevertheless, she rolled out of bed and headed into the bathroom to shower and face the day.

Trevor lay still, eyes closed. A prayer began forming in his heart. "Lord, this is so hard for me. I want to provide nice things for Carissa. I want to take care of her. And now she's the only one who even has a job. I don't want to think of the millions I gave up when I quit baseball, but this is hard for me, Lord. I need Your help."

Do you have food to eat and a place to live? Have I not given you a warm bed to sleep in, and the joy of a wife?

"Yes, Lord, You have provided," Trevor whispered, "but this is still hard for me."

As she came out of the bathroom, Carissa saw the pained look on Trevor's face. She didn't like living this way either. She liked having money to do the things she liked, not barely enough to pay the bills. And she knew that the inability to provide was weighing heavily on Trevor's heart. His whole life had been focused toward a lucrative baseball career, and now he was floundering, searching and not finding his new place in the world. It was hard to watch, to know what to say. To tell the truth, she would have loved to be taken care of by a wealthy baseball player. It didn't give *her* ego any strokes to make more money than Trevor. She wasn't interested in being saddled with the obligation of being the primary breadwinner. Whatever it was that God was doing in their lives, it didn't feel good. It felt as though it was *just enough*. Where were the *rich* blessings?

Trevor eventually found a job at Cedar Youth Services as a tracker, monitoring the kids' whereabouts in the community and whether they were going to school. It was a good job in that he had the ability to influence kids, but it didn't pay well. He was beginning to really worry about their financial situation.

Late one Sunday night he turned on the radio and began listening to *Bible Answers Live With Doug Batchelor*. He liked Pastor Batchelor's candor and knowledge of the Bible. As Pastor Batchelor finished with a caller, Trevor's mind wandered. He thought for the thousandth time about what he might do to better his life, to make more money, to buy a house—to be the man.

"Is it a sin to worry?" A soft-spoken woman had called in her question.

"Is it a sin to worry?" Pastor Batchelor repeated. "Well, it can be."

He had Trevor's attention.

"The Bible tells us that we should be 'anxious for nothing, but in everything through prayer and supplication' make our requests known to God [Philippians 4:6]." There was a pause as Pastor Batchelor seemed to be flipping through his Bible. Then he continued: "In the Sermon on the Mount Jesus says we're not to worry about what we'll eat or drink."

"Oh, yeah!" the woman's voice brightened.

"He tells us to seek God's kingdom first. And in Psalm 37: King David says: 'Do not fret.' So there's quite a bit in the Bible that tells us to trust God, to have faith, and to not worry. This doesn't mean that you've sinned every time you worry if you're going to make it to the next gas station."

The woman seemed to be grasping where Pastor Batchelor was going. And so was Trevor.

"God gives us practical sense that keeps us, say, from reaching out and grabbing rattlesnakes; but if we're living in a perpetual state of worry, then that is a sin. It's an attitude of not having faith."

A feeling of calm seemed to descend over Trevor. "Lord," he prayed, "I'm sorry I've carried the weight of worry around with me. Help me to remember to seek Your kingdom first, and let You take care of the rest. And thank You for meeting my needs."

Chapter 19

O dear God, please! Can't You make this happen?" Carissa flung the bathroom door open wide and threw herself in a heap of sorrow on the bed. Outside the window the buds were popping open on the trees, and squirrels were frolicking in the grass. Everywhere she looked new life was bursting forth. But the new life she most wanted continued to elude her.

Carissa and Trevor had been married a little more than two years. In that time they had bought a house, adopted a chocolate lab named Drake, and were doing OK at their jobs. Carissa worked for a non-profit organization that provided services for people with disabilities. Trevor worked at Christian Heritage, helping to place kids in foster care. They had formed a close friendship with many in their young adult Sabbath school class at church, especially Kelly and Becky Krueger. So much was going right for them now, but one thing most certainly was not: they couldn't get pregnant.

When Trevor got home from work, he found Carissa crying on the bed. "I'm still not pregnant!" she wailed, punching the pillows. "And it's all my fault!"

"No, no; that's not true," he soothed, taking her in his arms. "It's just not God's time yet. We have to trust Him."

"The doctor says I exercise too much, and I'm too thin," Carissa sniffled. "He says that's why I'm not getting pregnant. And you can tell me all day to trust God, but Trevor, let me tell *you* something." Carissa pulled away and looked at him with the full force of her erupting emotions. "God doesn't make any kind of sense! He lets all kinds of people who don't want babies get pregnant. He lets babies come into the world and be abused by mothers who didn't want them in the first place, and He can't find it within His plan to let *me* have a baby?"

Trevor pulled her closer. "Carissa, you know I can't speak for God. I can't explain every mystery, and I'm not going to try. But I *do* know that God hears our prayers. He knows our hearts, and He has a plan for our lives. I *know* we have to trust Him with this."

"OK," Carissa agreed finally. She leaned into Trevor and allowed him to pray for both of them.

☆ ☆ ☆

"I was so impressed by the sermon today," Ardyce said, setting the sweet corn on the table.

Trevor and Carissa had come over after church to share Sabbath lunch with Trevor's parents. Duaine sat quietly at the table, eating his food. He hadn't gone to church, and he wasn't sure that he'd have been impressed if he had gone. Listening to his wife and son blather on about points of doctrine or pieces of Scripture gave him a headache. All he wanted was to be able to sit in his own home with his own family and not feel like an outsider.

"Did you see that Shane Komine got called up?" Duaine interjected.

"Yes, Dad, I did see that." Trevor answered with an easy smile.

"Coulda been you," Duaine jabbed.

"Duaine, stop that! We were talking about the sermon at church today!" Ardyce reprimanded. When was he going to let Trevor off the hook about baseball? she wondered. It seemed as though Trevor's decision to quit baseball had happened a lifetime ago. In the time since, it was as though he had become a totally new person. Yet Duaine insisted on sulking in his own little corner of the world, licking his wounds and blaming Trevor, Carissa, and the church for all his misery. It was getting old!

Duaine accepted his verbal slap with a nod. Sometimes it was better just to sit back and listen to things you didn't understand. Obviously, his family wasn't going to start talking about a subject he *did* know something about. He had beliefs, of course, thoughts on the subject of God and faith. And he liked Christian music. But they were just flying around over his head with all these references to where things

171

were found in the Bible. He hadn't been raised in this kind of environment, and he didn't figure he was going to get any more comfortable with these kinds of lunch conversations now after all these years.

☆ ☆ ☆

"Happy birthday, Trevor!"

His coworkers at Christian Heritage were celebrating his twenty-ninth birthday with a noon-hour party, festooning his desk with balloons and trailing streamers from the ceiling.

"Blow out the candles and make a wish!" one of them commanded.

"You have to cut the cake, Trevor. You get the first piece," another said.

Somewhere under the streamers and celebratory debris Trevor's phone began to ring.

Pushing his cake plate aside, he picked it up. "Christian Heritage, this is Trevor."

"Trevor, I'm so sorry to bother you on your birthday, but your dad's not here right now, and I need to talk to somebody . . . The doctor says I have breast cancer." Ardyce's shock and grief poured over the phone.

"I'm coming. I'll be right there, Mom." Trevor put down the phone, offering his apologies as he ran from the room.

He let himself into his parents' home and found his mom in the kitchen.

"I can't believe this is happening to me," Ardyce cried, leaning her head against his chest.

"It's OK, Mom. We have to give it to God. He's in control, and we need to trust Him."

After saying a little prayer, Trevor added, "You're not alone, Mom. I'll be right here with you—whatever you need."

☆ ☆ ☆

Ardyce awoke to a gentle touch on her hand. "Hello, I'm Christie. I'm going to be your nurse today. How are you feeling this morning?"

"Pretty rotten," Ardyce admitted.

The nurse gave her a compassionate smile and continued asking a few more questions about her level of pain and needs for the day.

"Hey, Mom!" Trevor called, coming through the door. Seeing Christie, he stopped.

"Come on in!" Christie said cheerfully. "I was just leaving. Let me know if you need anything," she added, making sure Ardyce had the call button within reach.

"I feel so sick today," Ardyce said.

Trevor pulled a chair close to the bed and took her hand. "Let's pray, Mom. We can always ask God for comfort and strength. I know He's listening."

"Trevor, you have been my rock through this." Ardyce choked on the lump that was forming in her throat and threatening to become a full-blown bout of exhausted tears. "When I've needed you, you've been here. And I know I couldn't have said that about you two years ago. I just can't believe the change God has made in your heart."

"Well, any change is all by His power. I know one thing for sure: I'm powerless to change myself."

☆ ☆ ☆

Becky Krueger studied the pregnancy test carefully. Could it be a false positive? She wasn't ready to be pregnant yet. This wasn't part of the plan. She called to Kelly as she emerged from the bathroom, still holding the test. "Honey, I'm pregnant," she announced, then broke into tears.

Kelly was shocked, but he gathered his wife into his arms and patted her reassuringly. "Becky, this is a gift from God. Sure, it's a surprise, but children are a blessing."

Then, looking down into her face, he suggested, "Why don't we thank God for this gift and ask Him to help us open our hearts to having this baby sooner than we'd planned."

"How are we going to tell Trevor and Carissa that we're pregnant?" Kelly asked, thinking of their best friends from church.

"I think we should all go out together to Red Robin," Becky answered. "I love their fries, and it's a fun and festive place to share good news."

"Well, now, I'm kind of getting excited about this baby!" Kelly grinned.

"Me too!" Becky agreed, scrunching up her nose in a mischievous smile. Putting her arms around Kelly, she said, "And I'm glad you're the daddy."

☆ ☆ ☆

Carissa elbowed her way through the door and deposited a bagful of decorations on the table. She sank into a chair and surveyed the little pink bows and booties on the napkins she had just bought.

"I don't know how long I can keep on doing this," she told Trevor, tears welling up in her eyes. "It seems as if all our friends are having babies. It's been a year, Trevor! I've smiled and acted happy; I've put on all these showers and bought all these gifts for other people—and all the while I'm just praying that God will give us a baby, and He never does."

"I know you're disappointed," Trevor soothed. "I am too, but let's try not to be angry with God about it. We've got to have faith that He will give us a baby when it's right. God is the miracle worker. All we can do is have faith. He blesses us with things every day."

"I know you're right," Carissa said, "but I feel so bad anyway. It's as if there's a big hole in my heart, and God's not willing to fill it." Then brightening a little, she added, "But Becky and Kelly invited us to Red Robin tonight. We probably should leave pretty soon. At least we know *they* aren't likely to have a baby anytime soon. Becky told me they weren't even trying yet."

A half hour later Trevor and Carissa wound their way through the crowded front entry at Red Robin. Becky and Kelly already had a table and motioned them over.

"Hey, guys!" Carissa greeted them. "How's it goin'?"

"We're good," Becky smiled, looking up from her menu. Cocking her head to one side, she looked at her friend carefully. "Carissa, are you OK? You look as if you've been crying."

"I have been," Carissa said honestly. "It never seems like the right time to admit it, but I've been wanting to get pregnant for about a year now, and it's just not happening. I guess I lost it tonight before coming here. So many of our friends are getting pregnant . . . I don't know, it's just hard." Then forcing a smile, she brightened. "But I'll be OK—as long as you guys don't get pregnant I think I can hang on."

Becky and Kelly about broke each other's toes as they kicked each other under the table. Tonight was *not* the night to break their news to the Bullocks.

☆ ☆ ☆

Trevor stared at the Cornhusker season tickets his dad had gotten him for Christmas. He had tried so hard to connect with his dad. He still watched games with him on Sabbath, and going to games with him on Sabbath had seemed like the right thing to do for a long time. But so far Duaine hadn't softened in his resolve never to go back to an Adventist church. Trevor's efforts to share this time with his dad didn't seem to be doing any good. Duaine wasn't reaching back to him.

Something else concerned Trevor. Watching games on Sabbath just didn't put him in the frame of mind he wanted to be in on Sabbath. He'd find himself caught up in the excitement of a close game and realize that he'd forgotten it was Sabbath. It bothered him when that happened.

"Lord," he prayed, "please help me find some other way to bond with my dad. I love him so much."

He put the tickets into his pocket. He'd made his decision. He was going into downtown Lincoln to sell them.

☆ ☆ ☆

The Kruegers had invited Carissa and Trevor over for a quiet evening. As she moved around in the kitchen, Becky seemed distracted. They *had* to tell their friends about the pregnancy sometime, preferably before she began to actually show, but there seemed to be no good way

175

to do it. She noticed that the guys were locked into a tight conversation about *something*—Becky wasn't sure what—and Carissa had just gotten up to come to the kitchen to see if she needed any help.

Here goes, Becky thought. She knew she couldn't hold it in any longer. She looked at Carissa—and burst into tears.

"What in the world, Becky! What's wrong?" Carissa grabbed her friend into a tight hug.

"Oh, I'm so sorry, Carissa!" Becky sobbed. "I don't want to have to tell you, but I do have to tell you because it's not going away, and—" Suddenly she couldn't seem to make her mouth work.

From the other room, Kelly looked up and then took hold of Trevor's arm. "I think we need to go to the kitchen."

"Just say it!" Carissa pleaded.

"Well, I'm pregnant!" Becky blurted. "And I know how hard this is for you to hear, and I'm sorry. I'm really sorry!"

Suddenly Carissa was as teary and befuddled as Becky. She was happy for her friend—yes, happy! Swallowing hard, she said, "It's OK, Becky. You'll be a great mom, and I'm happy for you. Really, I am!"

Reclaiming their drippy wives, the men agreed it was time to give thanks for the gift of this unborn child, and time to ask again for God's best plan in God's time.

☆ ☆ ☆

Little Kent Krueger was born in September. And still Trevor and Carissa waited for the day that they might have happy news of their own. It had been almost two years since they had first hoped to have a baby.

After they visited Becky and Kelly and met the baby, they returned home and gravitated toward the couch, where they became a huddled mass.

"I don't think I could face this struggle to have a baby if it weren't for you, Trevor," Carissa cried softly into his chest. "You've encouraged me and been understanding. You haven't blamed me. And you've had faith when all I had was anger. I couldn't ask for a better husband. I just can't believe how much you've changed."

☆ ☆ ☆

Carissa had a feeling (wishful thinking, no doubt). Mother's Day was a couple days off (now, *there* was a holiday that could set Carissa to crying more than usual), and she couldn't seem to sleep. So in the early-morning hours she tiptoed out of bed, chastising herself all the way to the bathroom. What on earth made her think this time would be any different? This was the same eager expectation that had been devastated month after month. But maybe, just maybe, it might be different this time. She thought she felt a little different . . .

She closed the bathroom door softly. Could she stand another disappointment? She took the test and set it level on the counter. While she waited, she prayed. "O Lord, please give me courage to face the outcome."

Opening her eyes, Carissa looked. Then looked again. Was that the marking she'd seen every other month? She didn't think so! But she also didn't trust herself to read these things anymore. Trembling, she checked the paper insert from the box.

Through the misty fog of sleep Trevor heard someone calling, "Trevor, come here!" He forced his eyes open and willed his feet to move. When he stepped into the bathroom, he found Carissa on the floor, shaking, holding the test stick in her hand. She held it up to him and begged him to verify that she was right.

He did—and she was.

Sliding down onto the floor beside her, tears of joy running down their faces, they offered up a prayer of praise and thanksgiving to God.

☆ ☆ ☆

All this time their only "child" had been Drake, the dog, and each Mother's Day they had signed the cards to their mothers "From the three of us."

This Mother's Day they invited Ardyce and Rebecca to their house for lunch. At the end of the special meal they gave them their cards. As she read the card from Trevor, Ardyce basked in the warmth of her son's love. After years of prayers and, well, challenges, he was a steady, devoted son. She couldn't be more proud—but what was this? At the bottom it was signed "From the four of us." Four? Had they gotten another dog?

It took only a moment before Ardyce blurted, "Are you *pregnant?*"

Rebecca, who hadn't gotten to the end of her card yet, whirled around at Ardyce's exclamation and yelled, "What? What did I miss? *Are* you pregnant?"

The glow on Carissa's face was confirmation enough. "Yes! I'm pregnant!" she squealed.

Immediately the three women became a wiggly mass of huggers. Trevor looked on with a grin, Drake pounded a steady beat with his tail, and for that moment all was right with the world.

Chapter 20

The crowd was still a little thin as Trevor and Kelly entered Kauffman Stadium. As they walked past the concession stands the popcorn was popping and hot dogs rolled around on their sizzling path to nowhere. Off to the side, cotton candy swirled into glistening strands. In the distance a voice yelped, "Programs! Get your programs!"

If Trevor saw all this, he didn't comment. He kept a steady pace, heading for their seats on the third baseline. When they came to the short satellite arm that linked the concourse to their section of the stands, he slowed down just a little. There was always a moment when his breath caught in his chest as he stepped out of the cavernous shadows of the concourse into the brightness of the field. No matter how loud the music was playing at that moment or how tangled the crowd was in front of him, he'd stop and hear nothing at all. He was having that moment now.

Pushing forward, the pair found their seats. Then Trevor slipped away. As he watched him go, Kelly wondered what he must be feeling—or thinking. What does a man do when he comes face to face with "what if"?

Trevor angled around some people and trotted down the steps to the rail. Leaning over, he called catcher Carlos Ruiz and pitcher Yoel Hernández over to talk. They'd been his teammates from the Lakewood BlueClaws. Now they played for the Philadelphia Phillies, and here they were, warming up on the field at Kauffman Stadium, preparing to play the Kansas City Royals.

When Trevor returned a little later, Kelly looked at him for a moment. "You doing OK?"

"I'm fine," Trevor replied.

Out in center field the signature fountains of Kauffman Stadium came on, and everyone stood for the national anthem. Then the game began. In the bottom of the first inning left-handed pitcher Jamie Moyer took the mound for the Phillies.

Kelly slipped a look at Trevor again. A *lefty* was pitching for the Phillies. An *old* lefty. Kelly was sure Moyer was in his 40s. As his eye quickly scanned Trevor's face, however, he saw no sign that Trevor was thinking the obvious: *That should be me out there instead of that old man.*

Estaban German came to the plate for the Royals, and Moyer struck him out. *Well,* Kelly thought, *maybe Moyer will prove he deserves to be here. Maybe Trevor won't have to regret leaving after all.*

That didn't turn out to be the case. The Kansas City Royals lit Moyer up. After pitching only 3⅓ innings, Moyer had given up six runs. The Phillies brought in Ryan Madson, who took only two innings to give up three more runs. In came José Mesa. He gave up two more runs, and now Geoff Geary was running out to the mound. In a third of an inning Geary managed to give up *five* runs!

"How can you stand this?" Kelly blurted, shaking his head.

"OK, this is hard to watch," Trevor admitted. "I'm sitting here wanting to tell these guys what to pitch. Sure, I think I could get them out of the jam, but Kelly, even though I *am* feeling twinges of regret, they aren't regrets about reality. They are regrets about what I *wanted* the game to be. When I dreamed about playing major league ball I didn't dream about being lonely or tired or sore. There wasn't any truth to what I dreamed. And my dream wasn't going to come true, even if I did climb to the top."

Turning back toward the field, Trevor looked at the action on the mound. "What I mean is, the game is pure, but everything that encompasses the game isn't. I might wish I could have been out there pitching today, but I know that even if I *had* gotten the chance to save this game I'd still be unhappy. If I were still in the game I'd have the selfish blessing of still being in the limelight. As it is, I have the more peaceful blessing of knowing God and having Carissa as my wife."

When the game ended, the Phillies had lost 17 to 5. The Kansas City fans weren't even celebrating anymore. It's not all that fun to win in a rout. Trevor was mostly quiet too.

As they got into the car Kelly asked, "What are you thinking about?"

"I noticed a girl," Trevor said with a far-off look in his eyes.

Kelly wasn't sure he followed. "A girl you *knew?*"

"I don't know; maybe I knew her. She looked kind of familiar—that honey colored hair reminded me of someone . . . I think."

Kelly didn't say anything. He maneuvered the car out of the stadium parking lot and headed for Interstate 29.

"I hoped I wouldn't notice the girls today," Trevor sighed.

"Oh, c'mon!" Kelly laughed, "I noticed them too. Is it a problem to *notice?*"

"I suppose not—if all you do is *notice*," Trevor said with a flicker of a smile. "Speaking for myself, I do more than notice. For a long time baseball and girls went together for me. I was hoping that I could come enjoy some baseball today without girls being an issue. But I guess habits die hard, because I was lusting after them all day long."

Kelly and Trevor had recently been reading the book *Every Man's Battle: Winning the War on Sexual Temptation One Victory at a Time,* by Steve Arterburn and Fred Stoeker. Kelly knew that both Trevor and he really struggled with lustful thoughts.

"Well," he said after a silence, "I can understand that it was disappointing for you to find that your lustful desires were still there, but remember that this is a daily struggle. We have to ask God every day, ask in the moment, for Him to help us turn away."

"You're right," Trevor agreed. "Jesus died to save us *from* our sin, not *in* our sin. We have to be willing to walk away from the temptation. We have to surrender control to God and then obey when He tells us to run."

Kelly laughed. "Yeah. You still look like something is bothering you. Did something else happen at the game?"

"Kind of the same thing," Trevor replied. "I was just thinking that as fathers we have to teach our children to know the beauty and value of women. I don't think I've told you this before, but I was 13 when I lost my virginity. Ever since I was a kid, girls have been prizes to be won, rewards for being a hot baseball player—not people with character qualities and valuable thoughts." He shook his head sadly. "I've really struggled to change my view of women. Nobody taught me differently. I don't think my parents ever sat me down and had the sex talk with me. Parents need to talk to their kids and set an example of respect in their own marriages. Kids need that kind of guidance from the people they love and trust."

"You're making a good point," Kelly quietly answered, "I hope I can help Kent avoid these kinds of struggles."

"I hope you can too. Help him avoid the mess and guilt I had to face for so long. You know how my dad is always telling me I'd be set for life if I'd stayed with baseball?"

Kelly nodded.

"Well, Kelly, there isn't anything like big money to draw out all the women who want to claim their baby is yours. If I were in the big time right now I'd probably be throwing half my money away on paternity suits. I'll bet my dad didn't think of *that!*"

☆ ☆ ☆

Trevor had been unusually quiet for two days. Carissa sensed it had something to do with going to the game in Kansas City, but so far he hadn't said much. Finally, at breakfast she asked, "Did something happen at the game? You've been really quiet."

"No, nothing really happened." He reached out to take her hand. "I really love you, Carissa. I just wish I could provide better for you and the baby that's coming. And I know I could have made it to the majors. I know I could have made enough money . . ."

"Enough money so that you wouldn't need faith?"

Trevor smiled. "Yeah, I guess that much money."

"I like you better this way," Carissa said. "You're an amazing husband. You study your Bible, and you make me accountable. You lead me and help me and care for me. I couldn't ask for more."

"So you don't mind that I make nearly nothing?"

"Trevor, I think it's going to be hard to go back to working full-time after the baby comes, and I know I'm going to have to. So in that sense, no, I don't like this. But God knows I'd start depending on my money and not Him. If I had a lot of money, I'd be a mess. I think God is blessing us with just enough. He keeps us in a place where we remember that we need Him. And I'd rather be married to you, a man of faith, than have all the money in the world."

Chapter 21

Isn't this exciting?" Carissa squealed, giving her mom a hug. She and Trevor were preparing to leave for the hospital, where Carissa's labor would be induced.

Rebecca Lane squeezed her daughter back. Tomorrow would be BABY DAY! And she wasn't about to miss a minute of it. She was worried, though. Even though she'd seen a lot of change in her son-in-law, she still had her doubts that Carissa was going to have the support she needed during this very important event.

Carissa was a little nervous. What if, after all this waiting and praying and hoping and dreaming, there was a problem? Trevor reached over and took her hand. "Everything is going to be fine," he assured her. "I'm going to be there for you through all of it."

Rebecca had never seen Trevor so tender. *Is this the guy who used to make my daughter cry night after night,* she thought, *the one with a cocky strut and invincible air?*

Once at the hospital the couple settled in for the night, and Carissa received the medication that, hopefully, would have her in active labor by morning.

In the wee hours of the morning Carissa announced, "Trevor, I can't sleep."

"Are you uncomfortable? Do you need anything?" Trevor asked from his cot by the window.

"No, I just can't sleep," she said with a little giggle. "I have waited for this day for so long! A baby, Trevor! We're having a baby!"

Trevor came over to her bed and placed his hand on her swollen belly. "This is pretty amazing! God's been good to us."

☆ ☆ ☆

183

Carissa clutched at the side rails of the bed. She was sure she was going to die.

"Just relax, honey," a kind-faced nurse told her.

"I want an epidural—get me the epidural!" Carissa demanded loudly.

Rebecca and Trevor looked at each other and exchanged a look of understanding. Both knew Carissa had zero tolerance for pain.

"Well, I could check you again and see if you've dilated enough for us to give you the epidural," the nurse said patiently.

"No!" Carissa yelled. "That hurts too!"

"I'll come back in about a half hour, then," the nurse replied. "Maybe Dr. Milius will say you can have the epidural by then. But in the meantime, take deep breaths and concentrate on relaxing when it hurts, OK?" She disappeared through the door.

"I can't do this! I can't do this, Trevor!" Carissa wailed.

"Sure you can." His voice was warm and strong. "Do you want me to rub your back? I'm right here. Just breathe deep, like the nurse said."

It seemed like an eternity, but finally the anesthesiologist arrived with the epidural. In minutes Carissa had transformed into a happy, smiling woman. "Wow! I feel great! Bring it on!"

"That's great, honey!" Trevor grinned, mussing up her hair. "I guess you don't need *me* then."

"Yes, I do! You stay right here!" Carissa ordered.

The light mood held until the alarm on Carissa's blood pressure cuff went off. "What's that? What's wrong?" Carissa begged.

The nurse came in and quickly flipped off the alarm. "Your blood pressure dropped a little," she said calmly. "It looks like everything's OK, but I'll stay here for a few minutes and see if it happens again." When she was satisfied that Carissa was doing all right, she left again.

The minutes ticked by. Things seemed to be going slowly.

"You hungry?" Rebecca asked Trevor. "I think I'll go get a snack."

"No, thanks . . . You want some ice chips, honey?" Trevor asked Carissa

"Yes, please."

The hands on the clock crept forward. The nurse came in and left. The sun began to rise. The blood pressure alarm went off again.

The nurse came back—and waited, then left. Trevor stood up and stretched.

"OK, let's see how you look." It was Dr. Milius. "I'm just going to break your water, and then we'll need you to start pushing, all right?"

Suddenly the room burst into action. Things were raised and lowered on the bed. Lights came on. People appeared and started demanding that she PUSH!

"OK, Carissa, honey, it's time. PUSH!" Trevor said.

"You can do it! Take a breath! Push some more!" the nurse encouraged.

"That's good! PUSH!" Dr. Milius affirmed.

Carissa didn't even know who was talking to her anymore.

Then Dr. Milius informed them that the cord was wrapped around the baby's neck, and asked for the vacuum extractor.

Carissa shot him a frightened look. The vacuum extractor was *not* what she wanted.

Dr. Milius motioned for the nurse to wait. "OK, Carissa, on this next push I want you to push as hard as you can."

"OK," Carissa agreed. Anything to keep that vacuum thingy far away from *her* baby's head!

And with the next contraction, Gavin Duaine Bullock entered the world. Dr. Milius unwound the cord and let Trevor cut it. The nurses whisked Gavin away to lie under the warmer while they cleaned out his mouth and nostrils.

Than silence. And more silence.

"He's not crying!" Carissa said anxiously.

Trevor nodded. What could he do? If there was ever a time he wanted to control the outcome of something, it was now. Forget all the close games he'd pitched, all the pressure of getting out of a jam on the mound. This topped all of that. He wanted control. And he had none. Time stood still.

Then it happened. Rippling through the room came the unmistakable bawl of a newborn, registering fear and outrage at being forced from his cozy nest.

Trevor began to cry. "Thank You, thank You, thank You, God!"

☆ ☆ ☆

Back in the quiet of their room, Trevor and Carissa cuddled with their new son while the proud grandmas looked on, smiling. "I love you so much!" Trevor whispered, gathering the tiny body close. "I'd do *anything* for you." *Is this how God feels about His children, why He pursues them with His love, imploring them to come to Him when the struggles of life overtake them?*

At the nurse's prompting, Trevor had taken off his shirt so he could cuddle Gavin, skin to skin. He slowly paced the length of the room. As he passed the mirror over the sink he caught the reflection of the "T-Bull" tattoo on his shoulder, the red and green joker with baseballs hanging off the tassels of his hat.

Ardyce followed his gaze. "I'll still pay you any amount of money to get that thing removed."

"No, Mom," he responded firmly. "The tattoo is staying." Moving away from the mirror, Trevor placed a kiss on Gavin's head. "I want to remember where I've been, and where I don't want to go again."

Epilogue

Rob Avila advanced to the Class AA level in the Philadelphia Phillies organization, playing 10 games for the Reading Phillies in 2003 before retiring from professional baseball. Rob has a master's degree in physical education from Azusa Pacific University. In 2006 he became the head baseball coach for Palm Beach Atlantic University, a Division II Christian university. His wife, Beth, is the school's head volleyball coach. The couple has two daughters. They attend Grace Immanuel Bible Church, a nondenominational congregation, in Jupiter, Florida.

Ardyce and Duaine Bullock. Ardyce continues to be the secretary/treasurer of College View Seventh-day Adventist Church in Lincoln, Nebraska, where she has worked since 1988. She is now cancer-free and excited to be a grandma. Duaine retired as captain of the Lincoln Police Department's Narcotics Unit in January 2007, and is enjoying his new role of Grandad.

Texas A&M University Athletic Department Media Relations, 2008

Coach Rob Childress left the University of Nebraska in 2006 to become the head baseball coach at Texas A&M in College Station, Texas. He guided the Aggies in 2007 to a 23-win improvement, the biggest turnaround in NCAA Division I baseball history. He and his wife, Amanda, have a daughter and a son. Rob continues to stay in touch with Trevor.

Nate Lueders played baseball throughout his varied college experiences, playing for two years for Bellevue University, a top NAIA Division II baseball program in Nebraska. Now a social worker in Lincoln, Nate transports children who are wards of the state. He remains happily unmarried.

Ardyce Bullock Photo Collection, 2008

Lacee Rippee, 2008

Aaron Madsen pitched for two years at Seminole Junior College in Seminole, Oklahoma, and one year at Texas Christian University. He went on to graduate from the University of Nebraska with a degree in architecture. He endured a nagging inflamed ulnar nerve in his left throwing elbow throughout most of his collegiate career. He is currently a project manager with Geiszler Architects in the San Francisco Bay Area. He and his wife, Bobbi Lee, have two young sons.

Coach Guy Murray retired as head baseball coach at the University of Nebraska-Kearney in 2001. In his 29 years at the helm, the Lopers amassed 638 wins, 709 losses, and one tie, making him the school's most successful baseball coach. He was inducted into the American Baseball Coaches Hall of Fame in 1999. Guy still lives in Kearney with his wife, Sheryl, and occasionally attends Loper home games.

University of Nebraska at Kearney Sports Information Department, 1998

University of Wisconsin at Milwaukee Sports Information Department, 1999

Chad Sadowski advanced to the high Class A level in the Philadelphia Phillies organization. He pitched only two innings for the Clearwater Threshers in 2002 before an arm injury ended his pro career. Chad has worked as an assistant baseball coach at his alma mater, Cudahy High School, in Cudahy, Wisconsin, and has been a private hitting and pitching instructor. He plans to return to school for a teaching degree. He and his wife, Amy, are active members of WELS Lutheran.

Coach Dave Van Horn coached the University of Nebraska baseball team to their first two appearances in the College World Series in 2001 and 2002. He returned to his alma mater, the University of Arkansas, to take over head coaching duties in 2003. Dave has a 20-year coaching record of 823 wins and 379 losses. He and his wife, Karen, have two daughters.

University of Arkansas Media Relations, 2007